Contents

Before You Start

Before you begin this project, there are quite a few things that ought to be considered. For example, if you are buidling a PC to save money on a comparable pre-built system, you need to know the best place to buy the parts – buying them from your local computer store will result in a system that costs more, not less.

This chapter will give you all the information necessary to ensure you buy just what you need, and from the right places, in order to build a computer that is perfectly suited to your specific requirements.

Covers

Chapter One

Introduction

So, you want to build yourself a computer. OK then, take a good look at the following picture.

These are all the components required to build a computer system. As you can see, there are quite a few of them, and while putting them all together may seem a somewhat daunting prospect, this stage is actually relatively straightforward.

Building a computer also involves two other stages – buying the parts, and then having assembled them, setting up the system.

When you buy your parts, there are many factors to consider, and any mistakes at this stage can result in a computer system that, at best, is not what you really wanted it to be, and at worst, simply won't work. For example, the central processing unit must be compatible with the mainboard, and given the proliferation of mainboards, CPU socket types, etc, it is very easy to get this wrong.

Before you start, be aware that there are potential pitfalls with building a computer. Horror of horrors, it might not work – then you will be faced with possibly a major troubleshooting exercise.

To make sure you make the right decisions and do not end up with problems down the line, the book offers detailed buying guidelines regarding all the major parts in the system.

Having bought the parts, we then show you the correct way to install them. While this is not difficult, there are certain things you need to watch out for. A good example is the installation of the RAM modules. You need to be very careful when doing this as it is very easy to destroy them by incorrect handling. Liberal use of pictures helps to illustrate the assembly stage as clearly as possible. By the time you have finished, you should be looking at something like this:

Computers are modular in construction. This helps to make the assembly stage relatively straightforward.

Setting-up the system and getting everything to work, will, for most people, be the most difficult part of the job.

Finally, you need to set the system up. This will involve altering settings in the BIOS, partitioning and formatting the hard drive, and installing the operating system and device drivers.

Many, if not most, problems are encountered at this stage, so the book gives full instructions on how to access and setup the BIOS, and get the hard drive operational.

Finally, you will find a chapter on troubleshooting common problems; this will be very useful should you find your new system does not work as expected.

Store-Bought versus Self-Build

Self-build gives you the opportunity to reuse existing parts that may be perfectly adequate for your purposes. Why pay for something you already have?

Before you decide to take the DIY route and start spending your hard-earned cash on all the various parts, give some thought to the pros and cons. Building a PC yourself can turn out to be an expensive mistake if things go wrong. Also, remember there are good reasons for buying from a store. These include:

Time – self-build is going to take a lot longer than simply walking into your nearest store, buying a system off the shelf and then taking it home. To make it cost effective, you will have to spend time finding the cheapest suppliers of all the various parts, which will probably mean dealing with several different suppliers.

Effort – you have to actually build the PC, set it up and install the operating system.

Allow yourself plenty of time; someone who knows exactly what they are doing can assemble a PC from scratch, and have it operational in two or three hours. If this is you, then you really do not need to be reading this book.

However, if it is not, allow yourself a good day for the assembly and setting-up.

Aggravation – if the completed system does not work then you have to troubleshoot it. This will take more time, and if it turns out you have damaged a component during assembly, it will need replacing at extra cost. In addition, if you are unable to get the system working, you may end up taking it to a repair shop. All of this is going to involve more time and money. Buying from a store spares you all this aggravation.

Warranty – an off-the-shelf system will come with a warranty, whereas a self-built system will not. However, bear in mind that the warranty may not be all it's cracked up to be. There is a lot of competition between the various PC manufacturers and this has driven prices down to a level that shows little profit for them. Something has had to give, and in many cases, it is the after-sales service. While the manufacturers are obliged to honor their warranties, many of them take their own sweet time in doing so. This can mean a user being without the PC for weeks.

Pre-built PCs from major manufacturers often have proprietary parts. You have to go back to the manufacturer and pay exorbitant prices for any upgrades. When you build the PC yourself, you have generic parts that are cheaper to replace and upgrade.

The advantages of self-build are:

Cost – if you buy OEM parts (see page 14), and from the right source, your system should be cheaper than buying the ready-made equivalent. However, it must be said that the difference will probably not be as much as you might think, and if saving money is your primary motive, you may find it is simply not worth the bother.

Building your own computer allows you to "future proof" it to a certain degree. For example, you can choose a mainboard that can take a much more powerful CPU than the one you are intending to install. A year or so down the line, when the faster CPUs have dropped in price, you can then upgrade it. Another example is PCI slots. Some mainboards might only have three, or even less, limiting your options to upgrade by adding expansion cards. However, if your chosen mainboard has five or more then you should always have room for more cards.

Component Warranties – if you take the self-build route, you will at least have the warranties supplied with all the individual components. These are usually worth more than the PC manufacturers' warranties. Also, service from component manufacturers is usually much swifter and more reliable.

Quality – it is a fact that many pre-built systems, particularly at the lower end of the market, include parts of low quality. Typical examples are monitors, mice, and keyboards. Self-build allows you to choose good quality components that will give you a more reliable computer that is designed to last.

Design – buy a PC from a store and you will be buying things you do not need or want. For example, it may come with one of the latest video cards, which will add considerably to its cost. However, if you only use the PC for word-processing and email, you have wasted some of your money. By building it yourself, you will end up with a system that is tailored exactly to your requirements with no superfluous features or components. In this way you can cut costs.

Software – all ready-built systems come with an operating system pre-installed. In addition, there will usually be other software bundled with the system. However, this bundled software is often of dubious quality, and probably also well past its sell-by date. Much of it is useless to the buyer and so is money wasted.

A recent trend is for manufacturers to supply PCs with the operating system in the form of a "recovery disk", rather than an original CD. This is fine as long as the operating system works. However, should you ever need to reinstall it, or do a new "clean" installation, you could well run into problems.

There are few things as satisfying as tackling a difficult task and ending up with a successful result. Building your own computer definitely falls into this category.

While, with the self-build route, you may have the additional expense of buying the operating system, it will at least be an original copy that may be used as many times as necessary.

What Do You Want it to Do?

Having made the decision to build the PC yourself, you now need to make a list of all the parts required. This stage of building a computer is probably the most important, as any mistakes here will result in a PC that is not ideal (the whole point of the exercise), or that has to be subsequently modified at extra cost. However, before you can do this you must establish exactly what you are going to use the PC for, i.e. the applications you intend to run.

You then need to buy hardware (CPU, RAM, etc.) that will be capable of running these applications. While it is approximate, the table below will point you in the right direction:

Before you start spending your money on parts, think about what you are going to use the PC for, both in the present and the future. This will save you money in the long-term as you won't have to upgrade the computer before you should.

Application	Example	CPU	RAM	Disk Space
Operating System	Microsoft Windows XP Home Edition	300 MHz	128 MB	1.5 GB
Office Suite	Microsoft Office XP Standard	450 MHz	128 MB	400 MB
DTP	Microsoft Publisher	200 MHz	128 MB	180 MB
Graphics Editor	Jasc Paint Shop Pro	500 MHz	128 MB	80 MB
Games	Half Life 2	1.2 GHz	256 MB	4.5 GB
Media Player	RealNetworks Real Player	350 MHz	64 MB	52 MB
DVD Playback	Orion DirectDVD	233 MHz	70 MB	50 MB
CD Mastering	Roxio Easy CD Creator	200 MHz	64 MB	200 MB

Self-build gives you the opportunity to include things that you would not normally consider, or expect to find in a manufacturer's pre-built system. Read a few current computer magazines to see what devices are on the market. For example, if you watch a lot of TV, you might think about buying a TV tuner card that will allow you to watch TV and teletext on your PC. Some of these devices also allow you to use the PC as a video recorder.

While most programs don't need anything out of the ordinary, there are some that do. For example, the table above shows clearly that the game Half Life 2 will need plenty of system resources (a fact that applies to virtually all 3D games). Conversely, if all you want to do is word-process and play FreeCell, a basic system will be quite adequate.

Think of all the things you plan to use the PC for, what level of performance you need, and then buy your components accordingly. For the applications that really matter to you, get the best quality your budget allows.

Components You Will Need

 The components installed in your computer fall into two categories. These are as follows:

• *Essential – essential parts are those without which the computer will not work, or some aspects of it will not work, e.g. sound.*

• *Non-essential – these parts (known as peripherals) are add-ons, which provide increased functionality to the system, e.g. printers and scanners.*

There is also the issue of software, without which the computer will not be able to do anything at all, regardless of the hardware installed.

If you are working to a budget, there are some components on which you may be able to economize. Examples are the monitor, mouse, keyboard and video/sound systems.

Money saved here can be spent on more important parts, such as RAM, the CPU and the Power supply unit.

The following is a list of the hardware components you will need to build a basic computer system:

- Monitor
- System case
- Power supply unit
- Mainboard
- Central processing unit
- RAM module
- Hard drive
- Video card (see note below)
- Sound card (see note below)
- Floppy drive
- CD-ROM drive
- Keyboard
- Mouse
- Speaker system

NOTE: Many mainboards come with integrated sound and video systems. If you don't need high quality sound and video, these will be perfectly adequate.

Non-essential parts are known as peripherals and include:

- Modems
- Printers
- Scanners
- Removable media drives such as Zip drives
- TV tuner cards

OEM versus Retail

If you buy OEM parts, be aware that in many cases, you will be buying extremely limited warranties. There is also a risk of getting fake or sub-standard components. Only take this route if you need to save money where possible.

Having drawn up your list of required components, it is time to go shopping. One of your first decisions is whether to buy retail or OEM products.

OEM stands for "Original Equipment Manufacturer", and is a term used to describe a company that manufactures hardware to be marketed under another company's brand name. Typically, OEM products are sold unboxed and with no documentation or bundled software. Also, warranties offered can be limited. All this enables these products to be sold at a lower price.

The retail versions will be packaged, supplied with user manuals, registration cards and full warranties. Very often, the buyer will also get bundled software. Most importantly, retail products are guaranteed to be the genuine article – remember, there are many counterfeit products on the market.

If you want parts guaranteed to be of good quality, spend the extra needed to get boxed retail products. It could save you money in the long run, not to mention unwanted aggravation.

Another important factor is that of quality. All production lines produce a number of sub-standard products that nevertheless work. This is particularly so with silicon chips, which are to be found in virtually all PC components. In literally every production run, some chips will be superior to others, and these are the ones that will be packaged and sold at retail prices. Inferior chips often go the OEM route.

Therefore, if you are looking to build a high quality system, you will definitely need to buy boxed retail components.

If budget is your primary concern, then buy OEM. You will save money, but it could be at the expense of quality. As in all things, you get what you pay for.

If you do decide to buy any OEM products, make sure that you are not being conned into paying the full retail price. Be especially wary when buying OEM parts from a store.

Something else to be wary of when buying OEM, is that many retailers, computer stores in particular, will try to sell you an OEM component at the full retail price. No one who is computer savvy will fall for this, but many people are caught out and end up paying the full retail price for an incomplete and sometimes inferior product.

Boxed products will include things that OEM versions will not. For example, a boxed CPU will often include a heat sink and fan, plus a thermal strip. The OEM version will not.

Where to Buy Your Components

You have three main choices here:

- Computer stores
- Mail-order
- Online

When buying from a retail outlet, be wary of pushy sales staff that are quite likely to try to talk you into buying something that suits them rather than you. Also, take any technical advice offered with a pinch of salt – many of these people can be surprisingly lacking in knowledge regarding the products they are selling.

Computer Stores

Buying from a store is probably your quickest and safest option; you know where the store is if there is a subsequent problem and you can get there quickly. If a part is defective, you can simply take it back and exchange it for a new one.

However, it does mean getting off your backside, and does not offer the convenience afforded by the mail-order and Internet method of shopping.

Before setting foot in a retail store, bone-up on the technical details of the product in which you are interested.

If you do get a knowledgeable salesman, it will help you understand what he's talking about. You will also come across as computer literate, making it less likely that he will try to put one over on you.

It is a known fact that sales staff in many of these stores, particularly the large chain-stores, can be somewhat limited in their knowledge of computers. Any advice or opinions offered by these people should be taken with a pinch of salt and checked out before you part with your cash.

Also, be aware that they are salesmen and will often try to sell you a more expensive version of the item you are interested in. This is particularly likely if you do not come across as computer savvy. For example, you might inquire about an AMD processor, which is cheaper than its Intel counterpart. As the salesman is on commission, he might try to convince you that the Intel version is worth the extra with various statements such as, it provides better performance, etc.

You need to be clued-up about the latest versions of any products in which you are interested. Otherwise, you may end up buying last year's model and possibly paying today's price for it.

Manufacturers' web sites are the place to check for the latest products.

There is also the risk of being conned into paying the full price for outdated items. While, to be fair, this can also happen with mail-order and Internet companies, in practice, it is less likely, as these companies exist by undercutting the big computer stores and will take every opportunity to do so.

You will pay the highest price for your components in computer stores, as they have high overheads to cover.

Mail-Order

Mail-order is very convenient and allows the buyer to compare prices without having to trudge from store to store. In addition, you do not have to keep fending off pushy salesmen.

Mail-order catalogs and the Internet give you access to a much wider range of products than you are likely to find in any retail outlet. In addition, you will have no sales staff to keep at arms length, so you can browse at your leisure.

You will usually find that a mail-order catalog has a much wider range of products than you would find in any computer store.

Sales staff tend to be more knowledgeable about the products they are selling and will usually give you better advice than you would get in a store.

Prices will be lower than store prices and this is mail-order's main advantage.

When buying from catalogs, you ought to establish that the product is actually in stock before giving your credit card details. Some of these companies will take your money knowing it may be some time before they can deliver.

Disadvantages include time and distance. The company's headquarters could be several hundred miles away, so you cannot just nip down and get something. Delivery is done by courier, and it is quite common for goods delivered in this way to arrive in a damaged condition. This means more delays, and sometimes arguments, as to who is liable.

It is also not uncommon for goods to be out of stock. They do not want to lose your business, so rather than admit it and risk you going elsewhere, they will keep quiet about this and take the order. It is only when the goods do not arrive and you phone to find out why, that you will discover the truth. By this time though, they have your money. Again, to prevent you canceling the order and asking for a refund, they will tell you the goods are expected shortly and not to worry. If you are unlucky, it could be weeks before you actually receive your order.

Product specifications in mail-order catalogs are often minimal, and unless you have established from another source that the product in question will meet your requirements, you may end up with something that is not adequate.

Another drawback with mail-order products is lack of information. Whereas in a computer store you can get a lot of information from the box and associated promotional literature, not to mention actually seeing the product, details in many catalogs can be on the sketchy side.

The mail-order firm may send you the wrong item by mistake, which then has to be sent back. This can be particularly aggravating if it took a long time to arrive in the first place.

Online

The Internet really has revolutionized shopping, a fact that is particularly so in the field of computers and related accessories.

You will find web sites specializing in every single part of a computer system, such as power supply units, hard drives and monitors, etc. Sites such as www.pricewatch.com (shown below), will find the best online price available for any given product, saving hours of mouse clicking.

Check the satisfaction ratings of any web sites you are thinking of buying from before you place your order. You can do this through services such as www.resellerratings.com. Cheapest is not always best if the service is not up to scratch.

Many web sites offer products at seemingly bargain prices that do not actually exist. This is a common ruse to get you interested in the site. Sites selling bargain holidays and flights are typical offenders in this respect, and some computer-related sites use the same trick.

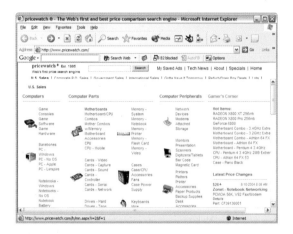

Most major computer retailers are now online and offer prices that are lower than in their retail outlets.

All computer manufacturers have their own web sites from which you can get detailed information about any products in which you may be interested. There are also sites that offer reviews on literally any component you are likely to need.

The Internet provides the best source of in-depth details and specifications regarding computer components. In particular, check out the manufacturers' web sites.

The big advantage to the consumer is price. Goods bought on the Internet will be cheaper than anywhere else.

In addition, online catalogs are often much more detailed in terms of specifications than mail-order catalogs.

In all other respects though, buying on the Internet is the same as buying mail-order. It all relies on courier and postal delivery, and is subject to the same limitations and restrictions.

Tools You Will Need

Assembling a computer does not require too much in the way of tooling; a toolkit, as shown below, is not necessary.

Do not go out and buy an expensive toolkit. The tools shown below are all that you will need.

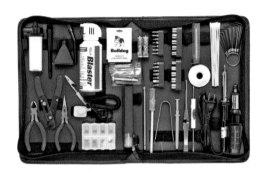

The following is all you are likely to need:

Screwdriver – one medium size cross-head screwdriver for screwing the mainboard into place and securing the drive units and expansion cards. You might also need a medium size flat-head for engaging the clips on an AMD CPU heat sink/fan assembly.

Needle-nose Plier – this will come in handy for removing or relocating mainboard and hard drive jumpers. If you do not have one though, a pair of tweezers will be adequate.

Cutter – for cutting cable ties to length. You will need these to bundle up the power supply unit cables in a neat fashion, so they do not interfere with airflow in the case. You will also need a supply of cable ties. These are available from any computer store.

Electrostatic Wrist Strap – this item is not essential, but is highly recommended. Static electricity in your body is a killer for your PC's circuit boards; this applies particularly to the RAM modules.

Flashlight – again, not essential, but once you have started installing components, it can become difficult to see clearly inside the system case.

A separate side-table, or similar, on which to put your coffee mug. With circuit boards and manuals littering the work area, you do not want to be spilling coffee all over the place.

Central Processing Units

You might think that choosing a CPU is a simple enough decision, i.e. the fastest one you can afford. However, this approach will probably result in you spending more money than you need to, and in any case, is no guarantee that you will end up with the right one for your particular requirements.

There are quite a few other factors that ought to be considered as well. For example, all CPUs are designed for a specific section of the market. Certain models come with features and enhancements, such as Hyper-Threading, which others do not.

This chapter will clear up some of the misconceptions regarding these devices, show you which section of the market you should be looking at, and explain associated terminology and technology. You will then be in a much better position to make an informed decision based on your actual needs, rather than marketing hype. Then we will show you how to install a CPU.

Covers

Chapter Two

CPU Manufacturers

Along with the mainboard, the processor is one of the most important parts in a PC, and more than any other, influences the speed at which it runs.

There are quite a few CPU manufacturers, the more well known being AMD, Intel, IBM, Compaq, SIS and Via. IBM and Compaq processors are aimed more at the business end of the market, while Via and SIS are better known for their chipsets, which are found on many mainstream mainboards.

Therefore, as far as the home-PC market and the self-builder are concerned, the choice comes down to Intel or AMD. Both companies make models for high-end, mid-range and low-end machines.

Intel

For a long time Intel dominated the processor market which could explain why its prices are higher than comparable offerings from AMD.

Its high-end CPUs are the Xeon and the Itanium, which are aimed at the Server market. These are seriously high-performance processors and are priced accordingly. For the self-builder they do not really come into the equation.

Of more interest is the Pentium 4. This is available in a range of speeds up to a current maximum of 3.6 GHz.

Courtesy of Intel Corporation

There are various versions of this chip – Willamette, Northwood and Prescott. Of these, the Prescott is top-dog with a faster Front Side Bus (see page 52) and a larger data cache.

The Willamette is bottom of the pile with the Northwood slotted in between.

Finally, there is the Celeron, which is essentially a budget version of the Pentium 4, and accordingly, offers lower performance levels.

AMD

With the introduction of their Athlon family of processors in 1999, Advanced Micro Devices (AMD), began a serious challenge to Intel's dominance of the market.

This has been due in no small part to the fact that AMD processors are cheaper than their Intel equivalents, while still delivering the same level of performance – indeed, many would say AMD processors perform better.

AMD's top of the range model is currently the Opteron, and as with Intel's Xeon and Itanium, is aimed at the business end of the market. Next is the Athlon.

This is the chip that will be of interest to the self-builder. The Athlon comes in several versions, one of the most popular being

the Athlon XP, which has been designed to take advantage of certain features of the Windows XP operating system. For this reason, it is an ideal processor to use with this system.

In general, the performance levels of Athlon CPUs are similar to Intel's Pentium 4.

AMD's budget CPU is presently the Sempron, which replaces the Duron – discontinued in 2002. This processor is intended to compete with Intel's Celeron.

The summary below gives a broad comparison.

There are two distinct markets for CPUs; the desktop market and the business market.

CPUs aimed at the desktop market are Intel's Celeron and Pentium 4, while AMD's offerings are the Duron (still available), the new Sempron and the Athlon.

For the business market, Intel offers the Xeon and Itanium, and AMD have the Opteron. These latter CPUs are extremely high-performance chips and are priced accordingly.

The only significant difference between CPUs from Intel and AMD is the price. In all other respects they are the same.

Intel		AMD
Celeron	equivalent	Sempron
Pentium 4	equivalent	Athlon
Xeon	equivalent	Opteron

Given that, performance wise, there is little to choose between AMD and Intel processors, the determining factor for most people is the difference in price.

Intel and AMD CPU Tables

For those of you who might like to examine the CPU market in a bit more detail, the following tables, while by no means exhaustive, will be a good starting point.

Intel market a range of their Pentium 4 and Xeon CPUs with a technology known as Hyper-Threading. This makes the CPU present itself to the operating system and application as two virtual processors. As a result, the CPU is able to handle two tasks simultaneously without any drop in performance.

Hyper-Thread CPUs require a HT Technology enabled chipset, BIOS and operating system. They are not recommended for use with Windows 2000, NT, 98, 98SE or Me.

You can find details of Hyper-Thread CPUs on Intel's web site at www.intel.com.

Intel Processors						
Processor	Core	Clock (GHz)	FSB (MHz)	Socket	L2 Cache	Date
Celeron	Willamette	1.8	400	478	128 KB	June 2002
Celeron	Northwood	2.1 to 2.2	400	478	128 KB	Nov 2002
Celeron	Northwood	2.3 to 2.4	400	478	128 KB	Mar 2003
Celeron	Northwood	2.5 to 2.6	400	478	128 KB	June 2003
Celeron	Northwood	2.7	400	478	128 KB	Sept 2003
Celeron	Northwood	2.8	400	478	128 KB	Nov 2003
Celeron	Prescott	2.4 to 2.8	533	478	256 KB	June 2004
Celeron	Prescott	2.9 to 3.2	533	478	256 KB	Aug 2004
Pentium 4	Willamette	1.4 to 1.5	400	423	256 KB	Nov 2000
Pentium 4	Willamette	1.6 to 1.8	400	423	256 KB	July 2001
Pentium 4	Willamette	1.9 to 2.0	400	423	256 KB	Aug 2001
Pentium 4	Willamette	1.4	400	478	256 KB	Sept 2001
Pentium 4	Willamette	1.5 to 2.0	400	478	256 KB	Aug 2001
Pentium 4	Northwood	1.6 to 2.2	400	478	512 KB	Jan 2002
Pentium 4	Northwood	2.4	533	478	512 KB	May 2002
Pentium 4	Northwood	2.6 to 2.8	800	478	512 KB	Aug 2002
Pentium 4	Northwood	3.0	800	478	512 KB	April 2003
Pentium 4	Northwood	3.2	800	478	512 KB	June 2003
Pentium 4	Northwood	3.4	800	478	512 KB	Mar 2004
Pentium 4	Prescott	2.8 to 3.6	800	478	1 MB	Mar 2004
Pentium 4	Gallatin	3.4	800	478	512 KB	Mar 2004
Pentium 4	Prescott	3.0 to 3.8	1066	775	2 MB	Early 2005
Pentium 4	Smithfield	2.8 to 3.2	800	775	1 MB	Mid 2005

This table shows just some of Intel's processors and is intended to give you an idea of what is available from this manufacturer. You will find that there are many versions and variations.

For a full list, together with detailed specifications, visit Intel's spec finder page at http://processorfinder.intel.com/scripts/default.asp?CHRID=483

There is a common misconception regarding the relationship between a CPU's clock speed and the speed of the PC. Many people are under the impression that if they replace their existing CPU with one that is rated at twice the speed, the system will be twice as fast. This is not so, however. While it will certainly be quicker and more responsive, applications will not open twice as quickly, data transfer will not be twice as fast, etc. You will only see the benefits of the extra processing power when you run an application that actually needs it. Instead of slowing to a crawl, as it might with the slower CPU, the system will effortlessly perform what is required.

When browsing the spec sheets of some of the newer AMD Athlon-64s, you may look in vain for the FSB speed. This is not an omission by AMD, however. These chips do not actually have an FSB – the CPU communicates directly with the RAM. The processor then interfaces with the rest of the system via a Hyper-Transport bus that has two separate channels, one in and one out.

AMD Processors						
Chip	Core	Clock (GHz)	FSB (MHz)	Socket	L2 Cache	Date
Duron	Morgan	1.0	200	A	64 KB	Aug 2001
Duron	Morgan	1.1	200	A	64 KB	Oct 2001
Duron	Morgan	1.2 to 1.3	200	A	64 KB	Jan 2002
Duron	Applebred	1.4 to 1.8	266	A	64 KB	Aug 2003
Sempron	Thoroughbred	1.5 to 2.0	333	A	256 KB	Aug 2004
Sempron	Paris	1.8	400	754	256 KB	Jul 2004
Sempron	Thornton	1.6 to 2.0	400	A	256 KB	Dec 2004
Sempron	Palermo	2.2	400	754	512 KB	Mar 2005
Athlon	Thunderbird	1.0	266	A	256 KB	Jun 2000
Athlon	Thunderbird	1.1 to 1.2	266	A	256 KB	Oct 2000
Athlon	Thunderbird	1.3	266	A	256 KB	Mar 2001
Athlon	Thunderbird	1.4	266	A	256 KB	Jun 2001
Athlon XP	Palomino	1.3 to 1.5	266	A	256 KB	Oct 2001
Athlon XP	Palomino	1.6	266	A	256 KB	Nov 2001
Athlon XP	Palomino	1.7	266	A	256 KB	Mar 2002
Athlon XP	Thoroughbred	1.2 to 1.4	266	A	256 KB	Apl 2002
Athlon XP	Thoroughbred	1.4 to 1.7	266	A	256 KB	Jun 2002
Athlon XP	Thoroughbred B	1.8	266	A	256 KB	Jun 2002
Athlon XP	Thoroughbred B	2.0 to 2.1	266	A	256 KB	Aug 2002
Athlon XP	Thoroughbred B	2.0 to 2.2	333	A	256 KB	Oct 2002
Athlon XP	Barton	1.8 to 2.1	333	A	512 KB	Feb 2003
Athlon XP	Barton	2.2	400	A	512 KB	May 2003
Athlon 64	Clawhammer	1.8	333	754	512 KB	Mar 2002
Athlon 64	Clawhammer	2.0	333	754	1 MB	Sep 2003
Athlon 64	Clawhammer	2.4	333	754	1 MB	Jun 2004
Athlon 64	Newcastle	1.8 to 2.4	800	754	512 KB	Jul 2004
Athlon 64	Sledgehammer	2.4	800	939	1 MB	Jun 2004

Rumors have it that the Athlon XP line is scheduled to end production in early 2005 with their place being taken by high performance Semprons.

CPU Terminology Explained

Here we will explain some of the terminology used in the tables on pages 22 and 23.

Core

CPUs are marketed as families, such as Intel's Pentium 4 and AMD's Athlon. Each family comprises many versions, each differing in terms of specifications. For identification purposes, each version is given a core name. Taking the Pentium 4 as an example, the different cores include the Northwood, Willamette, Prescott and Gallatin.

Clock

Clock speed refers to the speed at which a CPU runs, and is the most important indicator of a CPU's performance level.

FSB

The Front Side Bus is the data transfer channel between the CPU and RAM. The speed at which data is transferred is known as the FSB speed. This is another very important performance indicator.

L2 Cache

Level-2 cache is an area of extremely fast memory within the CPU. This memory bank is used to store frequently used data so it can be accessed much more quickly than if it had to be retrieved from slower RAM. The larger the L2 cache, the better the performance of the CPU.

The type of memory used for this purpose is extremely expensive, and therefore is one of the main determining factors in the price of a CPU.

AMD Performance Ratings

One aspect of AMD's processors that is the source of much confusion to buyers is their method of assessing CPU performance. Intel simply use the clock speed, i.e. a 2.6 GHz Pentium 4 CPU runs at 2.6 GHz. This is straightforward. An AMD 2600 Athlon might thus be expected to run at the same speed, but, in fact, actually runs at 2.1 GHz, which is a lot slower.

The performance levels of the two chips are, however, similar. The reason for this is that AMD makes up for the lower clock speed by having a higher instruction per cycle (IPC) rating.

Don't confuse the clock speed of a CPU with its FSB speed; these are very different specifications. Clock speed is the speed of the processor, while the FSB speed is the data transfer speed between the processor and RAM.

One of the main differences between CPUs that are otherwise similar is the capacity of the L2 Cache. This single factor has a major impact on the price of a CPU.

This means that, per cycle, AMD's CPUs do more than Intel's, with the result that overall performance levels are the same.

The problem for AMD is that most people rate the quality of a CPU by its clock speed. Given a choice between a 2.6 GHz Pentium 4 and a 2.13 GHz Athlon XP, they will go for the Pentium, wrongly assuming it to be a faster CPU. However, they both run at the same speed.

The performance rating system was introduced to clear up this misconception and indicates that the chip is equivalent in performance to an Intel chip with an identical clock speed rating.

There is a formula for working out the actual clock speed of an AMD chip from its performance rating, but an easier way is to refer to the table below:

AMD CPUs run at a lower clock speed than equivalent Intel CPUs. For example, an AMD Athlon 2000 with a clock speed of 1666 MHz, offers the same level of performance as an Intel Pentium 4 2.0 GHz CPU.

In recognition of the fact that consumers need more than just the clock speed to evaluate the quality of a CPU, Intel have recently introduced their own version of AMD's performance ratings.

This system replaces references to clock speed with a three digit "Processor Number". An example is shown below.

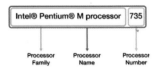

| Processor Family | Processor Name | Processor Number |

The Processor Number, i.e. 735, relates to the following specifications:

- Architecture
- Cache
- Clock Speed
- Front Side Bus

Perf Rating	Core	Speed
Athlon XP 1400	Palomino/Thoroughbred	1266 MHz
Athlon XP 1500	Palomino/Thoroughbred	1333 MHz
Athlon XP 1600	Palomino/Thoroughbred	1400 MHz
Athlon XP 1700	Palomino/Thoroughbred	1466 MHz
Athlon XP 1800	Palomino/Thoroughbred	1533 MHz
Athlon XP 1900	Palomino/Thoroughbred	1600 MHz
Athlon XP 2000	Palomino/Thoroughbred	1666 MHz
Athlon XP 2100	Palomino/Thoroughbred	1733 MHz
Athlon XP 2200	Palomino/Thoroughbred	1800 MHz
Athlon XP 2400	Thoroughbred	2000 MHz
Athlon XP 2600	Thoroughbred	2133 MHz
Athlon XP 2700	Thoroughbred	2166 MHz
Athlon XP 2800	Thoroughbred	2266 MHz
Athlon XP 2500	Barton	1860 MHz
Athlon XP 2800	Barton	2080 MHz
Athlon XP 3000	Barton	2166 MHz
Athlon XP 3200	Barton	2200 MHz

Buying a CPU

This really boils down to three main factors:

- What level of performance is needed?
- Cost
- Possible future requirements

Low-End System

If your requirements are basic, such as surfing the web, emailing, office applications, etc, you really do not need a fast CPU. A 1.0 GHz Duron or Celeron processor will give you more power than you are ever likely to use. Furthermore, the cost will be negligible.

However, regardless of how undemanding your applications are, if you run too many at the same time, a slow processor will struggle to cope. Also, bear in mind that you may, one of these days, discover a use for your PC that you did not anticipate, which does require more processing power. For this reason, it makes sense to invest in a bit extra processing capacity, should it be needed in the future.

Although they are available, given the relatively low price differential between a low-end CPU and a mid-range one, it really does not make sense to go for anything less than 1.5 GHz CPU.

Mid-Range System

Typically, a mid-range system, apart from the applications mentioned above, will also be used for a certain amount of game playing and will give good performance in this respect.

Word-processing and the like will be a breeze, and applications such as graphic and video-editing that would struggle with a low powered CPU, will present no problem, within reason.

It will be possible to multi-task (running several applications simultaneously), and in general, the system will be able to cope with most things asked of it.

You will need a CPU rated at 1.5 to 2.0 MHz, and if you are running Windows XP, an AMD Athlon XP CPU will be a good choice. A CPU in this speed range will also provide some spare processing capacity that will inevitably be needed as new and more resource-hungry applications hit the market.

High-end CPUs are very expensive and most people will never need the speed (processing power) they provide. Instead of spending $300 on a 3.6 MHz Pentium 4, buy a 2.0 MHz model for $70, and spend the $230 saved on other components.

High-End System

This is the ultimate, and with one of these you will be able to do literally anything that is possible to do on a desktop computer. If you are a hardcore gamer, this is the system that will get the best out of your games, particularly if you play online.

A high-end CPU is essential for serious game playing.

To achieve it, however, you are going to need a CPU rated from 2.5 GHz upwards, and this is where any budget you may be on will take a hammering.

Gamers and power-users wanting extreme levels of performance should look at Intel's "Pentium 4 Processor with HT Technology Extreme Edition".

This souped-up CPU will certainly deliver – at a considerable price. You could build a complete PC for less than this CPU costs.

However, it is a fact that unless you really want exceptional performance, the CPU is one of the components on which you can economize. With the majority of applications, there will be little noticeable difference, between say, a 1.5 and 2.0 GHz processor. It is only when you run resource intensive programs such as 3D games, or have many applications running simultaneously, that the difference will become apparent.

The price differential between a top-end CPU and a mid-range one is considerable, and your system as a whole may well benefit by spending more on extra RAM, a top quality power supply unit and a better video card.

Installing a CPU

The steps in this section show an AMD Athlon CPU being installed. The procedure is exactly the same, though, for an Intel CPU. Whichever you use, just remember that CPUs are fragile devices and successful installation will require a delicate touch.

The locking lever is part of the Zero Insertion Force (ZIF) mechanism which opens the socket's pin holes to accept the CPU.

Pick up the chip by holding it at the edges.

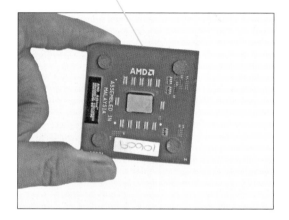

Intel's new 775 socket provides a more secure means of holding the CPU in place. The ZIF mechanism does not actually lock the CPU in place, and it is not unheard of for a large heavy heat sink to pull the CPU out of its socket.
  With the 775 socket, this cannot happen.

Lift the socket-locking lever to the ninety-degree position.

AMD processors have two diagonal corners and a gold triangle stamped on both sides of one corner. This is to ensure the CPU cannot be installed the wrong way round.

Intel processors have a gold triangle stamped on the front of the CPU and two pins removed on the business end.

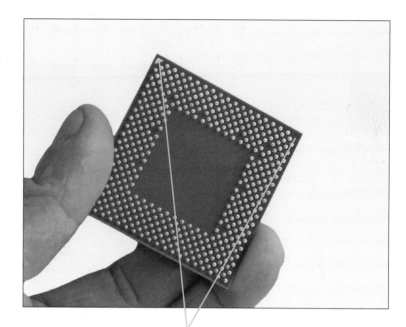

3 Align the two triangular corners of the CPU with the corresponding corners of the socket.

Pentium 4 mainboards employ a heat sink retention mechanism. Some boards come with this already fitted. Others, however, don't. If this is the case with yours, you will have to assemble and fit it yourself.

4 Drop the CPU into the socket.

Never try to force a CPU into its socket. If you do, you will bend, and possibly break, the pins. Wiggle it about slightly to line the pins up with the socket holes and it will then drop easily into place.

Before closing the locking lever, have a good look at all four sides of the CPU to make sure they are flush with the socket.

5 Close the locking lever.

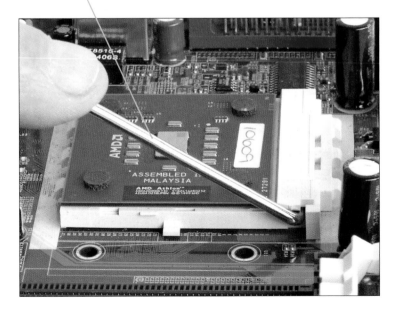

Fitting a Heat Sink and CPU Fan

The first step is to align the heat sink with the CPU. The bottom of the sink has a recess that engages with a corresponding lip in the socket.

Now you need to engage the locking clips. Holding the heat sink in place, engage the clip on one side over the plastic lug on the socket. You can do this with your finger.

3 Now engage the clip on the other side of the heat sink. This will require considerably more force and you will probably need a flat-head screwdriver to do it.

4 Finally, connect the fan to the mainboard's fan power supply. This will be a 3-pin socket labeled "CPU Fan".

Memory

Random Access Memory (RAM) plays a crucial role in a PC, and with the exception of the CPU, is the part that most influences its performance.

RAM comes in a range of types and versions, and picking the right ones can be a confusing issue for the uninitiated.

This chapter tells you all you need to know and will help you to make the correct choice.

Covers

Chapter Three

RAM Considerations

As with the CPU, the system memory (RAM) is a component that has a major impact on the performance of a computer system. You can install the fastest processor in the world, but without an adequate amount of compatible memory, all that processing power will do you no good at all.

Lack of performance in a computer system comes down to bottlenecks. One poor component in an otherwise highly-specified system, can drag all the good components down to its level.

Lack of sufficient, or poor quality RAM, is a common bottleneck.

Unfortunately, due to the many different types that are available (DDR, DRAM, SDRAM and RDRAM to mention a few), choosing the right RAM can be as difficult as choosing the CPU.

Increasing the amount of installed memory is probably the best and most cost-effective way to increase overall system performance. Even the slowest CPUs currently on the market are adequate for most purposes, so a faster model will make little difference. This is not the case with RAM though. Even a modest increase, say from 128 MB to 256 MB, will have a significant impact.

The first thing to realize is that all mainboards are designed for use with a particular type of RAM, so you must get a type that is compatible with the mainboard.

Then there is the question of RAM form factors. The form factor of any memory module describes its size and pin configuration. Typical examples are SIMMs, DIMMs and RIMMs. Buy the wrong one and it will not physically fit in the mainboard.

RAM modules also come in a range of speeds. SDRAM memory modules, for example, operate at speeds of 100, 133, 166 or 200 MHz. However, DDR (double data rate) SDRAM chips effectively double these speeds. A DDR module rated at a speed of 133 MHz will actually operate at 266 MHz. RDRAM operates at up to 800 MHz.

Therefore, the decision of which type of RAM to buy is far from clear-cut. To clarify the issue for you, we will briefly describe each of the more commonly used types on the market today.

Types of RAM

There are various technologies used in the manufacture of computer memory and the one currently in favor is Dynamic RAM (DRAM).

Most of the memory modules on the market are of the DRAM type or variations of it. The ones of interest to the self-builder are:

- Synchronous Dynamic RAM (SDRAM)

- Double Data Rate SDRAM (DDR SDRAM)

- Rambus DRAM (RDRAM)

Synchronous Dynamic RAM (SDRAM)

Until the advent of DDR SDRAM, this was the type most commonly found in PCs.

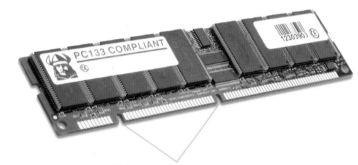

Edge connector cut-outs

With speeds of 66, 100, 133, 166 and 200 MHz, this module is supplied in the DIMM form factor with 168 pins. It is easily identified by the two cut-outs in the edge connector.

Although past its sell-by-date, this type of module is still found on older computers, and replacements of up to 512 MB can be obtained from parts suppliers.

The only reason a self-builder might be interested in buying one of these is if he or she are building a PC with an old mainboard that requires one. Other than that, there is simply no point, as DDR SDRAM modules are much faster and cost less.

Double Data Rate SDRAM (DDR SDRAM)

Currently, DDR (double data rate) SDRAM is the most commonly used type of computer RAM.

Very similar to its older cousin, SDRAM, DDR SDRAM operates twice as fast due to a technology modification whereby data is transferred on both the up and down sides of a clock cycle.

A DDR SDRAM module can be quickly identified by the single cut-out in the edge connector. The older SDRAM modules have two cut-outs.

DDR modules have a single edge connector cut-out

Identical pairs of DDR SDRAM modules can be used in a dual-channel memory setup. This requires a dual-channel mainboard, or more specifically, a dual-channel chipset on the mainboard.

The advantage is simple – you get twice the bandwidth, i.e. data transfer speed. Taking a pair of PC 3200 modules operating at a speed of 400 MHz as an example, the effective memory speed will be 800 MHz.

DDR SRAM comes in the following versions:

Model	Speed
PC2100	266 MHz
PC2700	333 MHz
PC3200	400 MHz
PC4000	500 MHz
PC4400	550 MHz

As with SDRAM, DDR memory is supplied in DIMM modules, the only physical difference being that they have 184 edge connector pins instead of 168.

Given that there is very little difference in price between the PC2100, 2700 and 3200 versions, the self-builder may as well go for the PC3200, regardless of whether the system being built is low-end or mid-range. Modules can have as high as 1 GB of storage capacity.

With regard the PC4000 and PC4400 modules, these are very high performance modules designed to provide the kind of performance that will only be of real interest to dedicated gamers. Typically, you will pay four times as much for one of these.

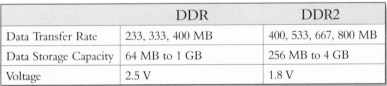

High performance DDR from Kingston Technologies

Double Data Rate 2 SDRAM (DDR2 SDRAM)

DDR2 is the latest incarnation of DDR SDRAM to hit the market and incorporates several new designs and specifications that result in much improved data transfer speeds. The following table shows the main differences between DDR and DDR2:

	DDR	DDR2
Data Transfer Rate	233, 333, 400 MB	400, 533, 667, 800 MB
Data Storage Capacity	64 MB to 1 GB	256 MB to 4 GB
Voltage	2.5 V	1.8 V

From this, we can see that maximum data transfer rates are doubled, while the maximum storage capacity of an individual module has increased to an enormous 4 GB. In addition, the power requirement is considerably less, which means less heat is generated.

At the time of writing, DDR2-400, 533 and 667 modules were just hitting the market; DDR-800 was not yet available.

As with all new products, DDR2 is extremely expensive, and also requires DDR2-compatible mainboards that are themselves expensive.

Rambus (RDRAM)

When it was first introduced, Rambus memory was touted as a revolutionary step up from SDRAM. Employing a special high-speed data bus called the Rambus channel, it offers effective data transfer speeds of 800 MHz.

Rambus offers very high performance levels, but at a seriously high premium. Hardware support, i.e. compatible mainboards, is also relatively thin on the ground.

This type of memory is not recommended for home-PC usage.

If you are prepared to pay the price, Rambus is well suited to applications requiring high-speed chip connections and high-performance memory.

As an illustration of this, Rambus memory is used in PlayStation and Nintendo games consoles.

However, Rambus memory has a high "latency" which, without going into details, to a large degree negates the extra performance derived from the high-speed bus. Thus, while there is a speed gain using a Rambus module, as opposed to a DDR SDRAM module, in reality, it is not worth the extra cost.

Rambus is very expensive – a 512 MB module will cost you five times as much as an equivalent DDR module.

While it is true that the new DDR2 memory costs a similar amount to Rambus, bear in mind that DDR2 is a new technology and so can be expected to be highly priced initially. Rambus, however, has been around for a long time now and shows no sign of coming down significantly in price. You can also factor in the high cost of Rambus-compatible mainboards that have to be manufactured to a higher design tolerance than those designed for DDR memory.

For a long time, Intel was the major advocate of the Rambus technology and pushed it for all it was worth. However, that support appears to have ended and consumers can draw their own conclusions from this fact.

Buying RAM

For guaranteed quality, buy branded memory from well-known manufacturers such as Kingston and Crucial. Avoid unbranded memory as you would the plague – if you don't, you may well end up with an unstable and error-prone computer.

When the time comes to make this decision, you should already have decided what type of system you want, i.e. low-, mid- or high-end, and chosen your mainboard and CPU accordingly. This is important, as to get the best out of your memory it must be compatible with the mainboard. You need to consider the following:

Manufacturer

Unlike the CPU, where the choice is essentially between Intel and AMD, both of whose products are high quality, there are a multitude of memory manufacturers.

As the memory plays a crucial role in the performance and reliability of a computer system, you must buy the best you can afford – memory is not a component on which to economize. Three manufacturers spring to mind here – Crucial, Corsair and Kingston Technologies. Buy your memory from any of these companies and you won't go wrong.

For typical computer applications, you need look no further than DDR SDRAM. Performance freaks will need to look at high-performance modules such as Kingston's Hyper X. Cutting-edge enthusiasts will be interested in the new DDR2 SDRAM.

Type

As we have already seen, Double Data Rate (DDR) SDRAM is the memory of choice for most at the moment. It is cheap, fast, and compatible with most mainstream mainboards. For low- to mid-level systems, it is the obvious option.

The high-performance DDR modules, such as Kingston's Hyper X and Corsair's XMS Pro series, will best serve high-end systems and dedicated gaming machines.

Some of the major RAM manufacturers have online buying guides, similar to those offered by Intel and AMD. These allow you to select your desired mainboard, and then show you which of the manufacturers' products are suitable for use with the board.

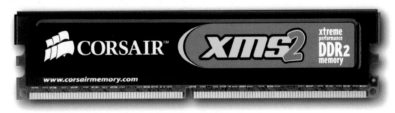

Courtesy of Corsair Memory

If you want your system to be as up-to-date as possible, you will need to bite the bullet and invest in the new DDR2 memory modules, regardless of the cost. This will also ensure your system is future-proofed as far as memory is concerned.

Speed

To get the best out of your memory it must be synchronized with the CPU, i.e. running at the same speed. For example, if you choose a DDR2 RAM module rated at 400 MHz, then you'll need a CPU with a 400 MHz FSB (see margin note). This is easily established by looking at the specifications.

Make sure the RAM you buy has a rated speed equal to the FSB of the CPU. If it is higher, you will have wasted some of your money as the system will be unable to utilize all the RAM's bandwidth, i.e. speed.

You will also need a mainboard that supports the same FSB. The easiest way to ensure you get this right is to look at the mainboard's specifications, which you will find at the relevant manufacturer's web site. Taking the Intel D915GUX as a random example, the specifications are shown below:

This board supports a CPU FSB of up to 800 MHz, so our 400 MHz CPU is supported.

If you make a mistake and install a RAM module rated at a higher speed than the mainboard and CPU are designed to handle, the RAM will still work but only at the mainboard's maximum FSB. You won't be getting the best out of it.

However, if you install a module rated at a speed lower than the FSB, this will create a bottleneck in the system as the RAM will not be able to keep up with the CPU. The result will be degraded system performance.

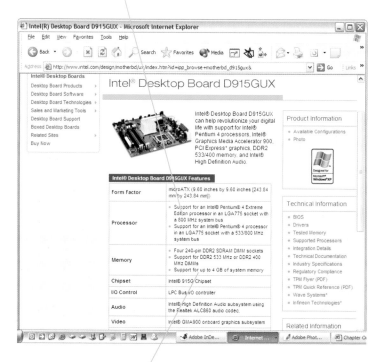

2 The specs also show you the type, speed and amount of RAM supported by the board. As we can see, DDR2 400 MHz modules are supported.

The maximum amount of RAM you can install is dictated by the mainboard and can be obtained from the board's specifications as shown on page 40. Most mainstream boards can handle up to 1 GB of RAM, which is overkill for the average user.

While it is often said that you can never have too much memory, you can go overboard with this and spend a lot more money than you really need to. For a low-end system, 256 MB will be more than adequate, while 512 MB will run most mid-range applications comfortably. Any more than this, will, ninety-nine percent of the time, never be used. It is only when running 3D games and applications such as video-editing, that you will benefit from more than 512 MB.

Also, don't forget that it is very easy to install extra RAM should you subsequently find a need for it.

Cost

DDR is good value. DDR2 is too expensive at present – wait until the price drops. Rambus is too expensive – full stop.

While an adequate amount of RAM is vital for good system performance, too much is simply a waste of money. The following is a realistic guide:

- *Low-end system – 256 MB*
- *Mid-level system – 512 MB*
- *High-end system – 1 GB*

DDR2 will soon be the standard for desktop PCs. However, the performance level it provides is overkill for the vast majority of current applications. If you want to be at the cutting-edge or future-proof the PC, go for it. Otherwise, DDR RAM will be quite adequate.

Type	Capacity	Price
DDR RAM	128 MB	$25
DDR RAM	256 MB	$45
DDR RAM	512 MB	$85
DDR RAM	1 GB	$215
DDR2 RAM	256 MB	$85
DDR2 RAM	512 MB	$180
DDR2 RAM	1 GB	$330
Rambus RAM	128 MB	$50
Rambus RAM	256 MB	$95
Rambus RAM	512 MB	$250
Rambus RAM	1 GB	$350

NOTE: The US dollar prices in the above table are approximate and are for comparison purposes only.

Installing RAM

Handling RAM Modules

As with CPUs, your body's electrostatic electricity can be lethal to memory chips. Ground yourself and then pick up the module by the edges, as shown below.

If you do follow the advice on page 18 and buy an electrostatic wrist strap, now is the time to use it. RAM modules are the components most likely to be damaged by incorrect handling. Just one careless touch is all it takes, so be warned.

RAM modules are also available with a heat-spreader. While these are intended primarily as a means of dissipating heat, they also provide the added benefit of protection.

Alternatively, rather than buy a module where the circuitry is exposed, go for one that comes with a heat-spreader, as shown in the example below.

Not only does this keep the module cool, it also protects the circuitry so you don't have to worry about how you handle it.

The first thing to do is open the plastic retaining clips on each side of the slots you are going to use.

The memory slots on the mainboard are numbered on one end – usually DDR1, DD2, DDR3, etc. If you won't be using all of them, fit the module (or modules), in the lowest numbered slots.

Align the cut-out on the module pin connector with the engaging pin on the slot.

If you've decided to install Rambus memory, be aware that any unused memory slots must be occupied by dummy modules. These are called Continuity RIMMS.

3 Holding the module upright (don't try and insert it from an angle), press down on both ends. You may need to exert some firm pressure here.

4 When the module is correctly seated, the retaining clips should close automatically. This doesn't always happen, though, and you may need to ease the clips shut yourself.

Mainboards

When you start looking at mainboards, you really do have a lot to consider. For example, this board, or more specifically, its PCI slots, will dictate how flexible the system is with regard to future upgrades and expansion.

You also need to consider your choice of CPU and RAM – the mainboard must be compatible with both, and capable of supporting their features, capacities and any special technology they employ.

Dual-CPU and 64-bit mainboards provide significant performance boosts, but are they for you?

This chapter gives you the low-down on all these issues and more.

Covers

Chapter Four

The Mainboard

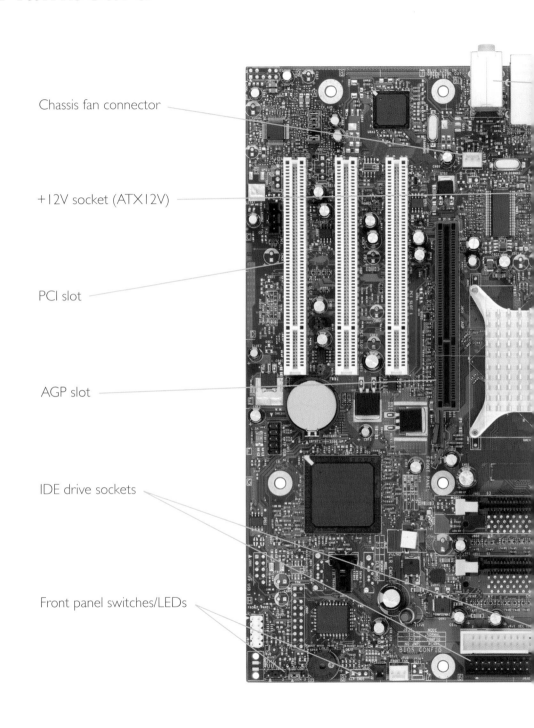

Chassis fan connector

+12V socket (ATX12V)

PCI slot

AGP slot

IDE drive sockets

Front panel switches/LEDs

Input/Output ports

CPU socket

CPU fan socket

Memory DIMM socket

PSU connection socket

Floppy drive IDE socket

What Does a Mainboard Do?

The Internet is a mine of useful information regarding mainboards. There are many sites that specialize in benchmark testing of new mainboards as they are released. These tests quickly identify a board's relative strengths and weaknesses. The reviews on these sites are well worth reading.

Using the human body as an analogy, if the CPU is the brain of a computer, then the mainboard is its central nervous system. Every single part of a computer system is connected, either directly or indirectly, to this piece of circuitry. This makes it the most important circuit board in the system.

Because of this, deciding which board to buy will be an important decision. Not only do you have to consider the features and quality of the board itself, you also have to think about how it will affect the other parts of the system.

Before we get into what you should be looking for in a mainboard, lets have a brief look at the more important of its functions.

- CPU and RAM – the mainboard provides sockets which enable these devices to be connected to the system.

- BUSs – these are basically "roads" and provide routes for the relaying of data.

- Chipset – this device is the interface between the system and the CPU. It organizes and controls everything in the system, and is an extremely important component.

There are dozens of companies involved in the manufacture of mainboards, and as with most products, whatever their nature, it usually pays in the long run to buy from a reputable and established company.

- Disk drive interfaces – these allow hard, floppy and CD-ROM drives to be connected to the system. Examples are EIDE and SCSI.

- Expansion slots – these enable a system to be upgraded by the addition of extra devices, such as video cards, modems and sound cards.

- Integration – many boards come with integrated sound and video systems. More recent boards also provide Bluetooth and Local Area Network controllers.

- BIOS – this chip controls a computer's boot-up routines and provides settings for many of the system's components.

- Ports – these are found at the back of the board, and provide a means of connecting peripheral devices such as printers, keyboards and mice.

Buying a Mainboard

Courtesy of Intel Corporation

AMD and Intel CPUs use completely different types of socket. They are not interchangeable – an Intel CPU will not fit into a mainboard designed for an AMD CPU and vice versa.

Before you can make a decision on which mainboard to buy, you must already have made some decisions regarding the components you intend to install in it, the CPU and RAM, in particular. For example, if you buy an Intel board and an AMD processor, it's not going to work.

Also, consider the operating system you intend to use. Quite likely, it will be Windows XP, in which case you ought to be aware that certain features in XP need to be supported by the mainboard's BIOS in order for them to work.

Let's have a more detailed look at the factors that will determine your choice of mainboard.

Central Processing Unit (CPU)

As far as CPUs are concerned, mainboards come in two main types – Intel or AMD compatible. Therefore, before you can

Windows XP incorporates some new technologies and features that must be supported by the mainboard in order for them to work. While older mainboards may well be available at knockdown prices to enable the retailer to shift old stock, and thus be tempting for the budget-conscious buyer, they may end up with a system that does not get the best out of XP.

Courtesy of Intel Corporation

decide on your mainboard, you need to decide whether you are going to use an Intel or AMD processor. They are not interchangeable – you cannot put an AMD CPU in an Intel mainboard or vice versa.

The choice of mainboard is further complicated by the fact that the various CPU families are designed to use a specific type of socket. Each of these sockets is physically different and will only accept the CPU for which they were built.

Therefore, you need to know exactly which processor you are going to use before you buy the mainboard, as the two have to be physically compatible.

Another thing to consider is the clock speed of your chosen processor. If it's not too high, say 2.0 GHz, most mainboards will be able to support it. However, if you intend to install one of the latest and fastest CPUs, you will also need one of the latest mainboards that has been designed to handle the extra requirements of these CPUs.

The best way to ensure you get the correct mainboard for your CPU is to go to the CPU manufacturer's web site. For example, at AMD's site (www.amd.com) you will find a system-building guide, as shown below:

The most foolproof method of matching the CPU to the mainboard is with the CPU manufacturers' system-building guides. Simply key in the required information and you will see which mainboards will be compatible with the chosen CPU.

AMD
1) Click Processors.
2) Click Support & Downloads.
3) In the menu at the left, click "System Building Guide".
4) Select your CPU and click "Build and Installation Guide".
5) On the right-hand menu, click "AMD .... Recommended Motherboards".

Intel
1) Click Personal Computing in the menu at the left.
2) Click "Build Your Own PC".
3) Click "Use the Motherboard & Barebones Selector Guide to find the right desktop board or preassembled system".

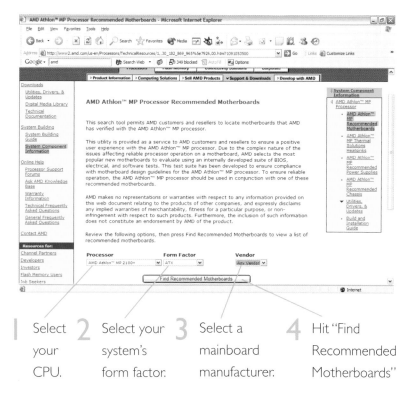

1 Select your CPU.

2 Select your system's form factor.

3 Select a mainboard manufacturer.

4 Hit "Find Recommended Motherboards"

You will now be presented with a list of compatible mainboards. Intel (www.intel.com) have a similar facility – see margin note.

Memory (RAM)

There are three things you need to consider in relation to mainboards and RAM.

- Can the board fully utilize the amount of RAM installed?

- Does the board support the rated speed of the RAM?

- Will the RAM modules physically fit on the board?

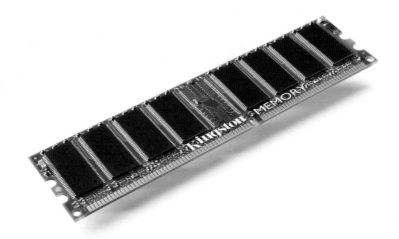

With regard to the amount of RAM, most mainboards of even half-decent quality will be able to support at least 512 MB, while many will support 1 GB. As it is extremely unlikely that anyone is going need any more than this, in most cases it should not be an issue.

As far as speed is concerned, make sure the mainboard supports the RAM's rated speed. If you make a mistake here, though, it is not critical. For example, if you put a stick of RAM rated at 266 MHz into a mainboard that only supports 133 MHz, the system will still work. However, the RAM will operate at the lower speed so you will not be getting the best out of it.

Unless you are using an old mainboard or memory module, you will have no problems fitting your RAM into the board. Most RAM modules now are sold as 184-pin DIMMs, and virtually all mainstream mainboards will accept these.

Chipset

A chipset is an integrated circuit found on the mainboard that controls the flow of data to and from key components of the PC. This includes the CPU, the system memory, the secondary cache, and devices connected to the system's buses, i.e. PCI slots and IDE channels.

A mainboard's quality and performance is directly proportional to that of the chipset. Amongst other functions carried out by this device are the board's integrated video and sound system.

Chipsets do not receive much attention – the focus is always on the CPU. However, these chips are a vital part of any mainboard and, to a very large degree, dictate its quality and features.

How do you, the buyer, tell the difference between a good chipset and a poor one. If you can make sense of all the technical jargon, read the specifications. You will need to know your stuff though – it is gibberish to most people.

A simpler way is to stick to a branded name. The major players in this particular market are Intel, Via and SIS. Go with any of these manufacturers and you won't be far wrong.

Front Side Bus (FSB) Support

The FSB of the mainboard must be at least equal to the FSB of the CPU and the speed of the RAM modules you intend to install in it. If it is lower, you won't get the best out of them.

The FSB frequency is the speed at which the CPU communicates with the mainboard and RAM and is also known as the External Clock Speed.

When buying the mainboard, you must ensure it supports the FSB speed of the CPU. If it doesn't, the CPU's performance will be severely degraded.

Many mainboards provide support for several different FSBs. While some of these boards will automatically configure themselves to the correct FSB, others will need to be manually adjusted. This is usually done in the BIOS during the setting-up procedure. Some (usually older) mainboards may require a jumper to be relocated on the board itself.

If you intend to buy an AGP video card, make sure the mainboard has an AGP slot. Not all do, so it's worth checking.

Expansion Slots

If you intend to install several expansion cards – modems, sound, video, and TV tuner cards being the most common – you must ensure your mainboard has enough expansion slots to accommodate them all. Most mainboards these days have several PCI slots and one AGP slot. Older boards will also have some ISA slots, a standard which is now obsolete.

Mainboards equipped with the "PCI Express BUS" are just hitting the market at the time of writing.

PCI Express is an extension of the common PCI BUS that doubles the data transfer rate of PCI, amongst numerous other benefits.

PCI Express will replace the PCI and AGP BUS within a few years, and cutting-edge enthusiasts, and those wishing to future-proof their system, definitely need to look at it.

The connection slots for this new BUS differ physically from PCI slots and so current PCI expansion cards are not compatible.

However, manufacturers are currently supplying both types of slot in their PCI Express mainboards so that they will be backward compatible with PCI.

At the moment, the only PCI Express products on the market are video cards from companies such as Abit and Chainforce.

However, many more companies currently have PCI Express products under development.

This photo of an old mainboard shows
3 ISA slots (black), 4 PCI slots (white) and
1 AGP slot (brown)

While a typical ATX mainboard can have up to six PCI slots, some will only have one or two, so check it out.

Some also come without an AGP slot, which you will need if you intend to fit an AGP video card.

Also, don't overlook the possibility that at some future date, you might want or need to install additional devices. You won't want to have to buy a new mainboard as well, so make sure your board has one or two spare slots for upgrading purposes.

Form Factor

As with the PSU and RAM, the size of a mainboard is specified by its form factor, an early example of which is AT. This standard has evolved into the ATX standard that is currently in favor. Developments of ATX include Mini-ATX and Micro-ATX. These are scaled-down versions that are used in smaller system cases. While Mini and Micro ATX boards are perfectly functional, they do have fewer PCI slots, which limits upgrading options.

The recommendation here is to go for a full-size ATX mainboard.

Integrated Sound and Video

Many mainboards come equipped with integrated sound and video systems that can substantially reduce the cost of building a PC.

However, as far as the self-builder is concerned, there are both pros and cons with these systems.

On the plus side, there are cost savings to be made. Not having to shell out for sound and video cards does save money. Plus, you won't have the bother of having to install them.

Another advantage is if you are looking to keep your system as small as possible, i.e. a desktop or mini system.

That's it as far as the pros go though; the cons outweigh them by far.

The quality of integrated sound and video is much lower than that provided by dedicated cards. This is particularly so with video, and if you are a hardcore gamer, forget this idea immediately.

Another disadvantage is that they rely on the CPU to do much of the work that a dedicated card, which has its own processor, would do. This can make a serious hit on overall system performance.

However, if you aren't looking for too much in these respects, and not everybody is, integrated systems will be perfectly adequate for the more mundane and undemanding computer tasks, such as word-processing, email, and even the occasional game, as long as you don't expect top-notch performance from it.

Integrated systems have improved tremendously over the last couple of years, and many now offer features that used to be the preserve of dedicated cards. For example, many integrated sound systems now offer support for 5.1 Surround Sound. Even gamers should find this good enough for their needs.

An inevitable side-effect of integrated sound and video systems is the negative impact that they have on overall system performance. This is because they rely on the system's CPU and RAM to do the number crunching.

Ports

A computer's ports are the assortment of sockets found at the rear of the system case. They are situated at the top-right.

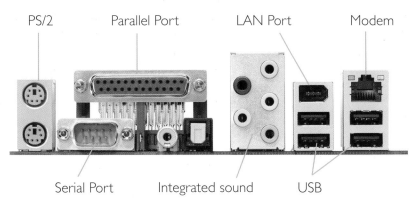

PS/2   Parallel Port   LAN Port   Modem

Serial Port   Integrated sound   USB

Most of these are standard and are supplied with all mainboards, unless integrated sound or video is not provided. In this case, you won't get the associated ports.

One thing that is not standard is the number of USB ports. While virtually all mainboards supply them – usually two – some boards will give you four, and with the current dominance of USB as a means of connecting peripheral devices, the more of these you have the better. Therefore, if you can find a board that meets all your requirements and also has four USB ports, go for it.

While on the subject of USB, this comes in two standards – USB1 and USB2. The difference between the two is data transfer speed; USB1 has a transfer rate of 12 MB/s, while USB2 transfers at 480 MB/s. This is considerably faster, and will make an appreciable difference to operations such as scanning, and downloading photos from digital cameras.

Therefore, the advice here is to get a mainboard that supports USB2 and supplies four associated ports.

Types of Mainboard

Dual-Processor Mainboards

Mainboards are categorized by form factors, the same ones, in fact, that are used to describe PSUs and system cases, as we have seen in previous chapters. However, we are thinking of something else here, i.e. mainboards that differ from the mainstream.

One example, is what's known as a dual-processor board, so-called because it uses two CPUs working in tandem. An example is shown below.

Do not confuse a dual-processor system with a dual-core system. Dual-processor means just what it says – two physically separate processors.

However, it is also possible to buy what is known as a dual-core processor, such as AMD's Opteron. This CPU has two processors contained within the same chip.

In practical terms, the difference between the two comes down to price and performance.

Whereas with a dual-processor system, nothing is shared – each processor has its own associated hardware, a dual-core system will share hardware such as the memory controller and BUS. For this reason, it is inherently less efficient, and its performance levels will thus be lower.

However, one dual-core CPU will cost a lot less than two separate CPUs, so the system will be cheaper.

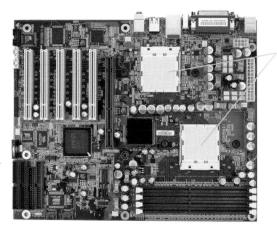

Dual CPUs add up to a lot of speed

Apart from two processors, these boards can support up to 4 GB of RAM, as well as the latest technologies. The result is speed – blistering speed.

Needless to say, setups like this are not cheap, but for those of you who can afford it, they are worth considering, particularly if you are likely to be running processing-intensive applications such as 3D CAD. In addition, you will be able to run any amount of normal applications simultaneously.

Add a top-end video card and hardcore gamers will think they've died and gone to heaven.

The downside, of course, is the price. The board alone will cost a small fortune, the amount of RAM needed to do it justice will cost a similar amount, and that's before you add in the cost of two processors.

64-Bit Mainboards

These are boards that have been developed to take advantage of the latest thing to hit the Desktop PC industry – namely 64-bit architecture processors. These CPUs can process 64 bits (instructions) at a time as opposed to the 32 bits of current mainstream CPUs, which obviously means they are twice as fast (theoretically).

64-bit technology is nothing new but until now has only been seen on server and mainframe computers. With the introduction of the Athlon-64 and 64FX processors, and Intel's extended Xeon, this technology is now available for desktop systems.

64-bit systems are not yet a reality for most as they require a 64-bit compatible operating system. One already exists for Linux users, but Windows fans will have to wait until the Windows XP 64-bit Edition becomes available. The release date for this seems to be somewhat "flexible". Sometime in 2005 is the latest projection.

64-bit systems are really only going to be of interest to those requiring extreme performance levels. The vast majority of home users will never need the speed and capabilities these systems will offer.

64-bit processors are backward compatible with current 32-bit software. However, this software won't be able to take full advantage of the benefits offered by 64-bit technology.

However, to fully utilize 64-bit architecture, 64-bit operating systems will be required, and, as usual, the software is lagging behind the hardware. At the time of writing, Microsoft have a 64-bit beta version of Windows XP available and are planning to release a final version. Other operating systems such as Linux already have 64-bit versions available.

Assuming you are happy with your present operating system though, you can still run a 64-bit processor as they are backward compatible with 32-bit systems. While you won't get the full benefit of the processor's capabilities, your machine will still gain an appreciable increase in speed.

As regards choosing which processor to go for – AMD's Athlon or Intel's Xeon – there appears to be little between the two.

Installing a Mainboard

Your system case may come with a sliding or removable side panel on which to attach the mainboard. The case we are using here does not; no matter, the procedure is the same.

You will probably also find some white plastic stand-offs. These screw into the side panel in the same way as the brass ones and then you clip the mainboard to them. Do not use these – the brass stand-offs offer a more secure fixing.

The first thing to do is find the plastic bag inside the case that contains the various fixings and rubber feet for the case to stand on. In this bag, you will find seven or eight brass stand-offs (shown opposite) to which the mainboard will be screwed. Put these to one side. At this stage you may as well fit the rubber feet to the bottom of the case; it's easier to do it now, when the case is empty.

Next, you need to remove the Input/Output shield from the rear of the case, as shown below.

The only advantage of a sliding or removable side panel is when the mainboard has to be accessed or removed from the system for some reason. Without one, you may have to first remove the PSU and disconnect all the drive unit cables.

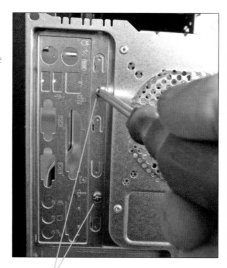

1 Remove the two retaining screws.

2 Remove the cover.

Now you need to establish exactly where to place the brass stand-offs. The side panel will have numerous threaded holes, combinations of which will accept mainboards of differing dimensions. Holding the board in place will reveal the ones you want. Screw the stand-offs into these holes. You can do this with your fingers and then tighten them up with a suitable spanner or a pair of pliers.

Make sure you screw in a stand-off to support the mainboard at each corner, plus two in the middle. If you don't, when you come to install your expansion cards and drive cables, the board will flex, and this can trash it.

Some system cases are supplied with a pre-installed PSU. If it is fitted horizontally at the top, or the case has a removable side panel, you should be able to install the mainboard without removing the PSU. If not, you will have to remove it before you can fit the mainboard.

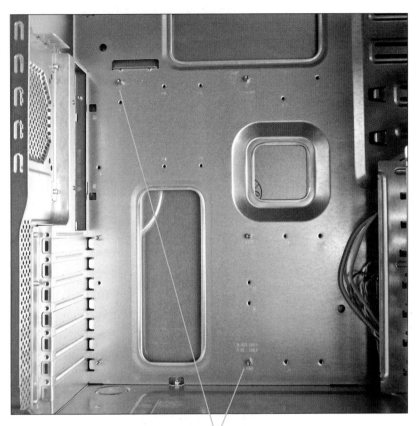

3 Screw the stand-offs in place ready for the mainboard.

4 Using the supplied screws, screw the mainboard into place. Don't over-tighten them – this is a PC we're assembling, not a car engine.

When screwing the mainboard down, make sure you use the screws supplied for the purpose. If you use screws from some other source, and the heads are oversized, you could short-circuit the board.

Don't forget to replace the Input/Output shield. It is there to prevent you from inadvertently poking things through, which can touch and maybe damage the mainboard. It can also prevent your inquisitive kids from getting an electric shock.

Finally, you must refit the Input/Output shield. If the one supplied with the case lines up with the mainboard's ports, then use it. You may, however, find that it does not, in which case you will have to use the one supplied with the mainboard. These are usually somewhat flimsy affairs that clip into place.

Input/Output shield supplied with the mainboard. While these are not as solid as the ones supplied with system cases, they are adequate

System Cases and Power Supply Units

System cases are important, as a well-designed model can make a significant contribution to the performance of the computer. From an aesthetic point of view, they also provide the self-builder with an opportunity to have a system that stands out from the crowd in terms of style.

Power supply units are much underrated components and the wrong purchase can prove to be a very costly mistake.

This chapter shows you what's available in the case market and which will be suitable for your needs. It also shows you what to look for in a power supply unit.

Covers

Chapter Five

Choosing the Case

The case is where all the main parts of the PC go and is a much underrated part of the system. Apart from protecting the components from the outside world, a well-designed case will keep them cooler than a poorly designed one. When buying a computer case, you need to consider the following factors:

Types of Case

Cases come in two main types – Tower or Desktop.

Desktop cases are the smallest and are often used with the monitor sitting on top. This provides their only real advantage – the relatively small amount of space they occupy. The downside is that

they provide limited potential for expansion, are awkward to work in and are difficult to keep adequately cooled. Typically, they will offer only two external drive bays and one internal drive bay.

Tower cases are by far the most common due to the extra internal space they offer. Not only does this allow more components to be installed, it is also easier to keep them cool due to the increased airflow.

Towers come in three main sizes – Mini, Mid and Full.

Mini-towers are similar in volume to desktop cases, but due to their design, are generally easier to work in and have more capacity. Currently, they are one of the most popular types for new PCs.

A full-tower case is the tallest size available, and provides the most flexibility with room for a large number of drives and other devices. Due to their size, these cases are usually placed on the floor.

Something to consider if you are thinking small is that desktop and mini cases provide very little in the way of maneuverability when it comes to installing the various parts. This can turn a relatively straightforward exercise into something much more difficult.

Computer form factors are standards that allow manufacturers to make their products physically compatible with other manufacturers' products.

The most common form factor currently in use is the ATX one. This will give you the widest range of options regarding compatible components.

Mid-towers are a compromise between mini- and full-towers, and are the ones found in most home-PC systems.

The main factor influencing your choice of case is the quantity of devices you intend to install. If you only need room for one hard drive, one CD-ROM/DVD drive and a floppy drive, and have no intentions of ever adding more, a desktop case will be adequate.

Anymore than this will require a mini-tower, which can have room for up to five external drives and four internal drives. Very few people are going to need more capacity than this. However, mini-towers are quite compact, and so can be very difficult to work in.

For this reason, a mid-tower is the recommended option as it provides all the capacity you are ever likely to need, is easy to work in and is not so big as to be obtrusive.

Form Factors

System cases are built to specific form factors that enable them to be correctly matched with the mainboard and power supply unit. This ensures that these devices will be physically compatible with the case.

ATX is the current form factor and the vast majority of mainboards, power supply units and system cases are designed to this standard.

Variations of ATX include Mini-ATX and Micro-ATX. Mainboards built to these form factors are basically cut-down versions, which allow smaller systems to be built.

Therefore, as far as the self-builder is concerned, a system case that conforms to the ATX form factor is what will be required. This standard is likely to be around for many years to come, and will ensure that there are no problems with compatibility issues, either now, or in the future.

Cooling Factors

All the parts in the case are designed to operate within a specific heat range. If they do, you will have no problems.

However, if your system overheats – and remember, you won't get any warning messages flash up on your screen – your parts will fail months, or even years, before they should do.

If you're only planning a basic system, i.e. one hard drive, one CD-ROM/DVD drive, a floppy drive and the minimum of expansion cards, cooling won't be something you need to worry about – the power supply unit and CPU fans will be sufficient to keep the system adequately cooled in any size of case.

However, if you are intent on a more sophisticated system that will include additional devices, each of which will increase the

temperature within the case, then extra cooling might well be required. The smaller the case, the more necessary this will be.

Unfortunately, there are no specific answers to this issue, so the advice here is to play it safe and buy a case with an integral fan or mounting points, which allow extra fans to be installed. These are readily available from computer stores and usually come with full instructions and mounting kits.

Noise Factors

The downside of extra fans is increased noise levels that can also be an important issue. If this is the case, for a few extra dollars, you can purchase fans that run silently. Another option is to buy a fan regulator or controller. These handy devices allow you to manually control the speed, and thus the noise levels, of up to four separate fans.

Many power supply units come with automatically regulated fans, the speed of which are controlled by the load placed on the PSU. These are another option for minimizing fan noise.

Alternatively, you can buy a sound-proofed case, or do the sound proofing yourself with a proprietary kit.

You can buy sound-proofing kits featuring pre-cut mats for certain case models. This will make fitting the kit a much speedier process, and should also result in a better job.

Many of the sound-proofed cases presently available are popular models from selected manufacturers that have been adapted by firms specializing in soundproofing. They are expensive though.

A much cheaper option is to do-it-yourself with one of the kits. These take the form of self-adhesive mats that you cut to size and then fix in place. Something to be aware of here, is that these mats can be anything up to twenty millimeters in thickness and will considerably reduce the internal dimensions of the case. Even in a mid-tower, you may well have difficulty in fitting the PC's components afterwards. In a mini or desktop, maybe not at all.

If you do decide to try one of these kits, get one with mats as thin as you can get away with.

NOTE: The manufacturers of some sound-proofing kits specify that you must also fit silent fans. This may make you wonder just how effective the kits are.

Another method of reducing noise is to replace the CPU's fan with a specially designed heat sink. These are also available to replace the fans found on high-end video cards.

Construction

Some cases have a better build quality than others. While virtually all are steel or aluminum, cheaper models can be somewhat flimsy. With these, you may also find that edges are not finished properly, with the result that you end up cutting or scratching yourself.

A very useful feature for the self-builder found on some cases is removable, or slide-out trays. These are particularly handy for accessing mainboards that would otherwise require other parts to be removed first.

Virtually all peripherals, such as scanners, external modems and digital cameras, use USB connections. Older systems had the USB ports (usually 2) hidden away at the back where they were awkward to access. It is becoming more common for cases to be supplied with USB ports on the front panel. This is something you should look out for when choosing a system case.

You might also consider buying a case with a lockable door that covers the front panel. This will considerably reduce the amount of dust that, over time, will infiltrate your CD/DVD drive unit's internal mechanism. It also provides an extra security option.

Alternatively, the door can be smaller and just hide the drive bays. For an added touch of luxury, you can even get cases where the door is motorized.

Aesthetics

When PCs first hit the streets, they all came in a rather bland beige rectangular box. While perfectly functional, they didn't exactly set the pulse racing. PCs bought from the large manufacturers still tend to follow this trend.

Computer style comes at a significant cost. Expect to have to dig deep, if looks, combined with quality, are important to you.

Nowadays, however, there is a huge range of cases in all colors and many different styles. These provide the self-builder with a perfect opportunity to have a computer that is a bit more interesting visually.

Courtesy of KingWin

Why settle for something dull when you can have one of these!

Most computer cases on the market are made of pressed steel. While there is nothing wrong with this – it is certainly better than plastic – anodized aluminum, which will be found in high-quality cases, is more efficient at heat transfer.

If you investigate this end of the market, you will find cases in brushed aluminum of all colors, clear and translucent acrylic, transparent side panels, and some with glowing LEDs that illuminate the inside of the case making it glow in the dark.

Apart from their looks, you will also get high-quality construction, usually in anodized aluminum, which is more efficient than steel at keeping internal temperatures low.

However, while these cases are stylish and attractive, they are very expensive when compared to standard cases – many of them will cost nearly as much as the parts inside them. Style comes at a price that will make a mess of your budget.

There are available though, many stylish enough cases at a reasonable price, as long as you are prepared to put up with a lesser quality of construction.

Power Supply Units

PSUs are one of the least interesting components in a computer system, but a good one is absolutely essential for a PC to perform reliably. They are also one of the most likely parts to fail, and when they do, they have a nasty habit of taking other components with them, RAM modules and CPUs in particular.

A high-quality power supply unit will be one of the most important purchases you make. Trying to save a few dollars here could cost you several hundred dollars further down the line.

For these reasons, a PSU is not one of the parts to economize on – if you do, it will cost you in the long run.

Factors you need to consider when buying a PSU are:

Load

The power supply unit you buy must be rated in excess of the combined wattage ratings of all the system's components. However, unless you are building a high-powered system with the latest processors and video cards, the figures in the guide opposite will be adequate in most cases.

PSUs are rated in Watts (W), and as far as desktop PCs are concerned, range from 250 W to about 500 W. Which one you will need depends on the total amount of power required by the parts in your system. As a guide, use the following table:

* Mini-tower or desktop – 300 W
* Mid-tower – 350 W
* Full-tower – 400 W

However, bear in mind that this is a rough guide and doesn't take into account the power requirements of high-end components such as Pentium 4 and AMD Athlon CPUs.

A more accurate way of determining what you need is to refer to the following table:

It is important to get a PSU that will handle your system's power requirements and still have a bit to spare. This gives you the option to expand the system in the future without also having to buy a more powerful PSU.

Component	Power Required
AGP video card	50 W
PCI card	10 W
IDE hard drive	20 W
SCSI hard drive	35 W
Removable disk drives	25 W
Floppy drive	5 W
Case/CPU/Video card fans	2.5 W
Mainboard	35 W
64 MB RAM	5 W
Pentium 4/AMD Athlon CPU	80 W
Older CPUs	35 W
LEDs	1 W

Do not judge the quality of a PSU by its wattage rating. This is a common mistake, similar to rating speakers by wattage. The best guide for the uninitiated is to buy from a reputable manufacturer.

This table shows the maximum power (approximately) needed for all the individual parts in a computer system, and will enable you to work out with a good degree of accuracy what PSU your system will need in terms of wattage. Whatever figure you come up with, get a PSU of a higher rating. For example, if you calculate you will need a 350 W PSU, get one rated at 400 W. There are two reasons for doing this.

Firstly, PSUs work best with a bit in hand. Running one at full load is not recommended if you want it to last any length of time. Secondly, if you decide later to add an extra device to your system, you will have enough power available to run it.

Protection

Good quality PSUs have circuitry that will prevent damage to other components in the system should problems occur. These protection circuits monitor the voltage, current and heat levels of the PSU, and if any of them exceed a designated level, the PSU will automatically shut down.

It is essential to make sure your chosen PSU incorporates protection circuitry that will shut it down when problems occur. Otherwise, it will eventually blow and you may well lose many of the other parts in the system as well.

Protection circuits are an extremely important feature, as all PSUs, no matter how good, will eventually fail. When they do, they are quite likely to take other components with them – most commonly the mainboard, RAM and CPU.

Good PSUs also offer protection against voltage surges in the external AC supply.

Cheaper PSUs do not offer any protection and should be avoided. The output voltages of these units also tend to fluctuate, particularly under heavy loads, which can be the cause of general system instability such as crashes and sudden reboots.

When making your choice, study the specifications and make sure they include protection circuitry.

Form Factor

The new Pentium 4 and Athlon based processors draw a large amount of current from the power supply. To help provide this extra power, a new ATX12V standard has been developed. If you have one of these processors, make sure the power supply unit is ATX12V compliant.

As with system cases and mainboards, all power supply units conform to a form factor. You must ensure that the form factor of the PSU you buy matches that of the case and mainboard. The ATX standard is the one you will need.

The only exception to this will be if you are planning to use a Pentium 4 or AMD Athlon CPU. Both of these processors draw an unusually large amount of power in comparison to earlier CPUs. Because of this, a new ATX12V standard has been developed. With either of these processors, you will need a PSU that conforms to this new standard.

Cooling

Look for a PSU that also incorporates a second, under or side mounted fan, particularly if you are building a high-powered system. This will help enormously to keep the system cool.

A good PSU will not only keep itself cool, it will also help to cool the other components in the case. All PSUs have a rear mounted fan that draws cool air in from the front of the case and expels heat from the back. Better models will also have an under, or side mounted fan, as shown opposite, which increases the airflow, and thus the level of cooling.

External Power Supply

Power surges are also commonplace on telephone lines. Apart from breaking your dial-up Internet connection, they can also damage your modem. Unless you have broadband, consider buying a telephone line surge protector.

While on the subject of power, you might also want to consider the AC supply to your PC. The vast majority of people never give this a thought – it's always there, it always works, so what's there to think about?

Well, actually, quite a lot. AC power supplies suffer from a range of faults, which can, and do, cause problems with PCs. These include:

- Blackouts
- Power surges (spikes)
- Line noise
- Over voltage
- Frequency variation

There are others but these are the ones which most affect a PC. Power surges (spikes) cause most damage, and in worst case scenarios such as lightning storms, can fry a PC completely. Usually though, you won't even be aware of them, as, typically, they have a duration of less than 0.001 seconds. They do, however, cause PCs to lock-up and crash. Furthermore, voltage spikes have a cumulative effect and over time will cause components to fail well before they should do.

In the event of a close proximity lightning storm, switch the computer off and disconnect it from the mains. Otherwise, you may end up with a pile of charred plastic and silicon.

AC power supply faults are also a common cause of data loss.

To eliminate these problems, the following devices are available:

- Surge Suppressors
- Power Conditioners
- Uninterruptible Power Supplies

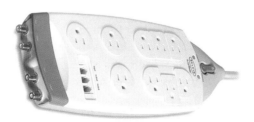

Courtesy of Belkin Corporation

Surge suppressors iron out any momentary increases in the supply voltage, thus ensuring that the input to the PC's PSU is at a constant level.

As with all your PC's components, it pays to investigate a surge suppressor's specifications before handing over the cash. A good model will also be capable of removing line noise and distortion in the AC signal, thus delivering a "clean" signal.

Surge suppressor protection is rated in Joules; this being the amount of energy that the device is designed to handle. The higher the number, the better the level of protection. A figure of 500 to 600 Joules will provide adequate protection for the home user.

Power or Line Conditioners work by filtering the signal to eliminate fluctuations and electrical interference that can cause

Courtesy of Belkin Corporation

noise. They also provide voltage surge protection and are a step up from surge suppressors. This is due to the more efficient way they clean up the AC signal. Not surprisingly, however, they cost more, and can also be bulky in size.

Uninterruptible Power Supply units provide the best form of protection and are more commonly found in office and corporate environments where data protection is critical. Apart from surge suppression and power conditioning capabilities, they also have a battery that will maintain power to the computer system in the event of a blackout. This allows ample time to save work in progress and close systems down until power is restored.

Courtesy of Belkin Corporation

For home users, a good surge suppressor that also has line-conditioning capabilities is the device to go for.

Installing a Power Supply Unit

Slide the PSU into position, using the shelf as a guide.

When sliding the power supply unit into position, take care not to make contact with the mainboard. This is something that's very easy to do, and while it probably won't cause any damage, it just might.

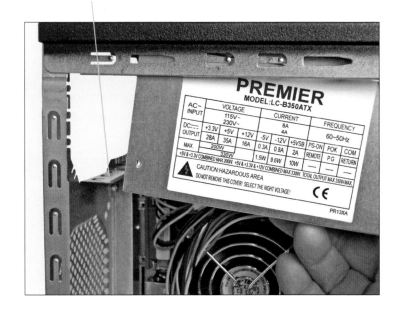

2 Supporting the PSU at the front, screw it to the rear of the case with the supplied screws.

When you have installed the power supply unit, remember to check that the voltage selector (if there is one) is set correctly. Also, make sure that the PSU's on/off switch is in the "on" position.

3 From the jumble of PSU connectors, disentangle the largest one. This is the power supply for the mainboard.

The PSU has four different connectors. These are:

Mainboard Power

CD/Hard Drive Power

Floppy Drive Power

ATX 12V

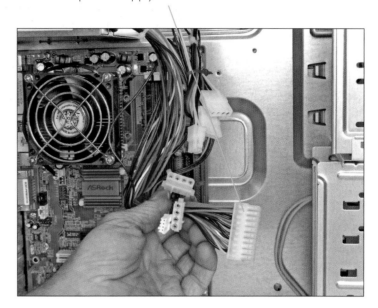

4 Locate the mainboard's power socket (this will be a large white socket) and plug in the supply from the PSU.

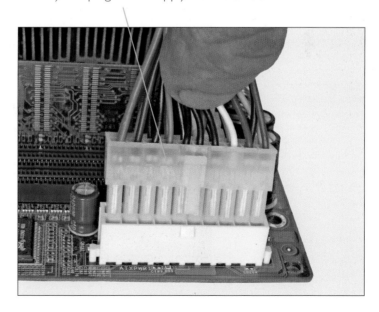

Case Connections

Finally, connect all the various case switches and LEDs to the mainboard. You will find these in a bank of connectors, usually at the bottom-right of the board.

It's very easy to get these connections wrong as the labeling on the mainboard is very small, and so can be hard to read.

In addition, the labeling on the cable connectors is often different, which doesn't help either.

While the following is not guaranteed to be the same as on your system, it will give you a guide:

1) *The P LED connector powers the case power LED and connects to the PLED pins.*

2) *The RESET SW connector powers the reset switch and connects to the RESET pins.*

3) *The HDD LED connector powers the hard drive LED and connects to the HDLED pins.*

4) *The POWER SW connector powers the case on/off switch and connects to the PWRBTN pins.*

5) *The SPEAKER connector powers the case speaker and connects to the SPEAKER pins.*

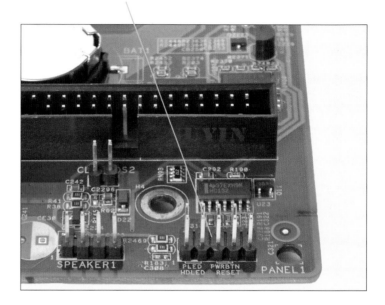

2 Connect the speaker, LED and switch cables to the mainboard.

Video Systems

To many people, the video card is one of the most important parts in the computer, and along with the CPU, it is certainly the most hyped.

This chapter cuts through the hype and slick marketing, to demonstrate that while 3D video is essential for certain applications, for most it is not.

Should you decide to buy one, however, there are many things you need to consider and these are explained in the following pages.

Covers

Chapter Six

Computer Video Systems

Integrated video has a much more pronounced effect on general system performance than integrated sound. However, on a reasonably specified system, the effects are relatively minor.

A computer's video system is responsible for converting the stream of binary 0s and 1s from the CPU into an intelligible picture that is then passed on to the monitor.

Two types of video system are used:

- Integrated video

- Video cards

Integrated Video

Integrated video is produced by a chip incorporated in the mainboard. This is the type of video system commonly supplied by manufacturers of cheaper systems, as it negates the need for a separate video card that would add to the cost of the system.

However, as video processing needs a processor and plenty of memory, and integrated video, typically, doesn't have either, it has to to rely on the system's CPU and RAM to carry out these functions. The effect of this is that the system as a whole takes a performance hit.

Unless you are a gamer or into graphic-intensive work such as 3D computer aided drawing (CAD), a good quality integrated video system will be perfectly adequate.

Also, as this type of system is primarily about cutting costs, the quality of the video produced has traditionally been on the poor side, and usually, only capable of producing two-dimensional displays. 3D video, such as games, has always required the use of a dedicated video card.

However, things do seem to be improving on this front, and many mainboards now on the market have integrated video systems that include 3D capabilities.

It is a fact though, that even these are only good for basic 3D reproduction, and will often still require screen resolution and color depth to be substantially reduced in order to get reasonable performance. They are not a serious option for the dedicated gamer.

However, if all you want is a basic system for office functions, multimedia and email, etc, integrated video will be quite adequate, and will save you the cost and bother of buying and installing a video card.

Video cards are much the same as CPUs regarding pricing. Every six months or so, a new batch appears on the market at a premium price that is out of most peoples' price range.

Fortunately, this drives the price of earlier models down to a level that is much more affordable. Unless you want a cutting-edge system, the advice here is to buy a card that is six months to a year old. You will pay much less than you would for one of the latest models, while the difference in performance will be negligible.

Remember, also, what we said at the beginning of the book about hardware technology advancing at a rate with which software cannot keep up. This is particularly true of video cards, and even models a year and more old, have capabilities that many of the latest games and applications are not able to fully utilize.

Many video cards come with integrated applications such as DVD decoding and TV tuners. If you are in the market for one of these cards, it makes sense to get something extra for your money.

Video Cards

A video card is a circuit board that plugs directly into the mainboard, usually via a special socket known as an AGP slot. It handles both the 2D and 3D requirements of a computer.

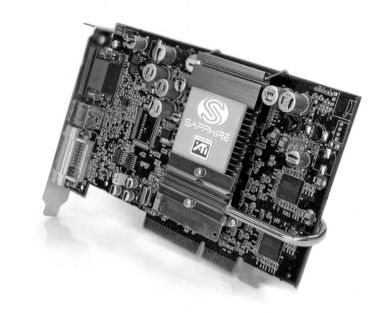

There are two main types of video card – the much touted gaming cards familiar to most of us, and workstation cards.

Gaming cards are designed specifically to get the best out of today's resource-intensive 3D games, to which end they have their own processors and memory. This leaves the system's CPU and RAM free to do the more routine and mundane tasks required of the computer. These cards often come with extras such as DVD decoding facilities, TV tuners and TV-out sockets that allow the display to be transferred to a television set.

Workstation video cards are intended for heavy duty stuff, such as 3D CAD applications, and can supply seriously high resolutions up to a massive 3840 x 2400. While 3D is catered for, they also offer exceptional 2D performance, which is usually far more important in a business environment than 3D.

2D versus 3D

On a day-to-day basis, for the majority of users, good 2D performance is of far more importance than 3D. While an integrated video system will give you reasonably good 2D, a video card with a quality, high-speed RAMDAC chip, will improve 2D performance greatly. This is why power and corporate users, who have no need for 3D, will always have a high-quality video card in their system.

It is all too easy to be taken in by the hype surrounding video cards and lose sight of the basics. While there is no dispute regarding the importance of 3D video, it is a fact that it's only critical to hardcore gamers and a handful of other applications. For most PC uses, and hence users, good 2D video is actually the more important of the two.

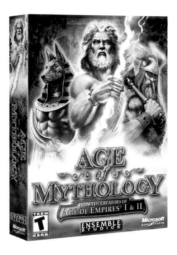

You'll need 3D video to play games such as Age of Mythology, but do you play them often enough to justify the cost of an expensive video card?

The minimum you want from a RAMDAC chip is a speed of 300 MHz. For really excellent 2D performance, look for a speed of 400 MHz.

Before you get sucked in by the slick marketing, ask yourself what you spend the majority of your computing time doing. Is it playing 3D games, or more mundane stuff such as basic Windows operations, office applications, email and web browsing, etc?

If it's the latter, then you need to be more concerned with your computer's 2D capabilities. They are the type of things that 3D has little effect on, whereas 2D does. Good 2D performance will improve image quality, text will be sharper, and basic things such as window manipulation will be quicker.

While all video cards are excellent at 3D reproduction, there are some that are not so good when it comes to 2D. The part of the video card that has the most influence on 2D performance is the Random Access Memory Digital to Analogue Converter (RAMDAC) chip. Before you buy any video card, look at its specs, and if the RAMDAC speed is less than 300 MHz, look elsewhere. The faster the RAMDAC, the better the 2D display will be.

Buying a Video Card

We will concentrate here on gaming cards; workstation cards are really a different entity and are extremely expensive – up to $2000 for a good one, which will be beyond most peoples' budget.

Workstation video cards can cost $2000 and more. The level of performance they provide, and features such as massive resolutions, will never be needed by the home user.

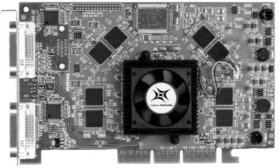

The Parhelia workstation video card from Matrox

Courtesy of Matrox Graphics Incorporated

When buying an AGP video card, make sure it supports the latest AGP speed of x8. For it to operate at this speed, x8 also needs to be supported by the mainboard.

When shopping for a video card, you need to consider the following:

Advanced Graphics Port (AGP)
Video cards plug into a special slot on the mainboard known as the AGP slot (see pages 46 and 53). This is a high-speed bus designed specifically for use with these cards. However, you can also get PCI video cards that plug into one of the PCI slots. These cards will operate a lot slower though, so you need to make sure your mainboard has an AGP slot (not all do), and that the video card you buy is an AGP version.

Look for a video card with at least 128 MB of memory. There are, still, older cards on the market offering 68 MB and even 32 MB.

Memory
One of the most important components on a video card is its memory. Almost all video cards made today come with either 128 MB or 256 MB of DDR SDRAM; budget cards will have less.

The more memory the card has, the better its performance, both 2D and 3D.

However, top-end cards with 256 MB of memory are extremely expensive, and you must consider whether you are likely to need the high level of performance that these cards provide.

Those of you wanting to keep abreast of current technology need to look at the new breed of PCI Express video cards that have recently appeared on the market.

PCI Express is a new type of system bus that is expected to replace the PCI bus over the next few years. Its main advantage is greatly increased data transfer speeds. However, to use a PCI Express device, you will also need a PCI Express mainboard.

Remember, also, that as this technology is new, at present there are few PCI Express mainboards around – a fact that also holds true for hardware. However, don't let this put you off; PCI Express mainboards will also be compatible with PCI for quite some time to come.

For most applications, a card with 128 MB of memory will be perfectly adequate. The performance differential between a 128 MB card and a 256 MB card is not usually that great, especially when running 2D applications, or games at moderate resolutions.

There is also the issue of what type of memory the card uses. Most cards presently on the market use DDR memory, but the latest ones are now using DDR2, and even DDR3. These latter ones are extremely fast, and if you want to be at the cutting-edge, are what you will be buying. They are, however, also very expensive, and should only be of interest to gamers and power-users.

Video Standards

There are two video standards that your video card must support – Direct3D and OpenGL.

These are very similar application program interfaces for manipulating and displaying 3D objects, and their purpose is to provide programmers with a way to develop 3D programs that can utilize whatever video system is installed in a PC. If you intend to buy a mid- or high-range card, this won't be an issue, as the vast majority of video cards support both of these standards.

However, if you are thinking of buying a budget card, or plan to use an old one, then it is worth making sure that the card in question does have Direct3D and OpenGL capabilities.

RAMDAC

We mentioned this on page 78: the RAMDAC is a chip on the video card that has a major influence on the card's 2D performance.

What you are looking for with regard to this device is speed – the higher the MHz figure, the better. Anything over 300 MHz will be fine, while 400 MHz will give you superb 2D performance.

Unfortunately, you won't find this specification mentioned anywhere on the card's packaging; the manufacturers are more interested in touting 3D capabilities. The best way, and in many cases the only way, is to look up the card's specs on the manufacturer's website.

Ports

Video cards come with a range of input and output ports, the number of which depend on the quality of the card. Budget cards will probably only have one – the VGA output to the monitor. Better cards will also have some, or all, of the following ports:

- Digital Video Interface (DVI)
- Video-in/Video-out (VIVO)
- Dual VGA

VGA Port   VIVO Port   DVI Port

It is not essential to have a DVI-equipped video card in order to use an LCD monitor. All LCD monitors will accept an analog signal from the video card, but will have to convert it to digital form themselves. This procedure will result in some loss of signal quality, however.

If you have a spare monitor, consider getting a video card with dual-VGA outputs. This will enable you to run both monitors at the same time, which can be very useful in certain situations.

CRT monitors are analog devices, and so the video card has to convert the PC's digital signals to analog before passing them to the monitor. This is done via the blue 15-pin VGA port.

LCD monitors, however, need a digital signal, and to cater for this many video cards now have a DVI port. If you are planning to use a LCD monitor, it will be handy if the video card has one of these – see margin note opposite.

VIVO ports allow you to hook up the PC to other video devices such as a television set, which can be useful for game playing or if a larger display area is needed. It is also possible to connect a VCR to this port to record stuff from the PC, or to export analog video to it – handy for digitizing those old VHS holiday movies.

Some cards also have two VGA outputs. This is known as dual-video and allows you to run two monitors from the same card. This can be useful in many situations; a writer, for example, can have his word processor open on one screen and his reference material open on the other.

Before you buy your video card, consider whether any of the above features may be of use to you, and if so, make sure the card has the appropriate port.

Physical Dimensions

Many of the top-end video cards are serious pieces of circuitry and by this, we don't just mean specifications, we mean big, as in take up a lot of room. This is further compounded by the also serious cooling systems these cards require.

A video card with two massive heatsinks, one on each side, plus a fan, making it an extremely bulky device

When fitted into the AGP slot, these cards will often completely block access to the nearest PCI slot, which means your mainboard will effectively have one PCI slot less. There are also a few cards that not only use the AGP slot, but also use the adjacent PCI slot. Again, effectively, you are one PCI slot short.

If you are intending to buy one of the top-end cards, don't forget to check the size of the card when planning what other expansion cards you are going to install. If you don't, you might just find yourself a slot short.

Power and Heat Issues

Power and heat are only issues if you are buying at the top end of the video card market.

The more features packed into a video card, the more power required to run it. You need to consider this when purchasing the power supply unit. You may, for example, find that you will need a 400 W PSU instead of a 350 W version – the extra 50 W to cover the power requirement of the card.

Furthermore, all this power generates lots of heat. While the card's cooling system will keep it cool, this heat will raise temperatures in the system case. Because of this, you may need to install extra fans.

Extras

Many video cards come with useful "extras" that can help to soften the impact on your wallet.

TV tuners are popular PC add-ons and allow you to watch television in a resizable window. While these can be purchased as a separate device, buying a video card with one built-in is a cheaper option. This has the added benefit of freeing up a PCI slot that would otherwise be needed for the TV tuner card, not to mention the bother of installing it.

DVD decoders are another common extra supplied with video cards.

DirectX

DirectX is an API that enables programs to be written without knowing exactly what hardware will be used to run the program. In particular, DirectX lets multimedia applications take advantage of hardware acceleration features supported by video cards.

Many software applications, particularly 3D games, are written around a specific version of DirectX and require it to be installed on the PC to function properly.

The video card must also support DirectX, so make sure that the card you buy supports the latest version of it.

As a rule, the amount of heat generated by a video card is directly proportional to its cost. The more expensive the card, the greater its processing capabilities; the inevitable by product of which is heat – lots of it.

Many video cards currently on the market do not support the latest version of Microsoft's DirectX. If you buy one of these, you may find that many of the latest games will not run properly. So be sure to check this out.

Installing a Video Card

At the bottom-rear of the system case, you will see a number of blanking plates adjacent to each slot on the mainboard. Remove the one next to the AGP slot.

2 Remove the board from the anti-static bag, holding it at the edges.

3 Slide the video card into the AGP slot and press it firmly home.

Some AGP slots use a mechanism to keep the board in place. Designs vary according to the manufacturer. The purpose of these mechanisms is to prevent the often bulky video cards from working loose in pre-built systems while they are being shipped.

4 Screw the face plate at the edge of the board to the chassis.

Don't forget to secure the board by screwing it to the case chassis. Unsecured components can work themselves loose over time.

...

5 Take the VGA cable from the monitor and plug it into the video card's VGA port at the rear of the PC.

You must tighten the screws on either side of the VGA plug. These secure the plug and will prevent it from working loose over time.

When connecting the VGA cable to the PC, make sure you connect it to the correct video output. If you are using integrated video, it connects to the blue socket at the mid-left of the case. If you are using a video card, it connects to the card's VGA socket.

If you are using the video system integrated in the mainboard, the VGA cable must be connected to the mainboard's VGA socket. This is the blue 15-pin socket.

Monitors

When it comes to buying a monitor, you basically have two choices – Cathode-Ray Tube (CRT) or Liquid Crystal Display (LCD). Each has its pros and cons and this chapter will explain what they are.

There are also several specifications which determine a monitor's quality and its suitability for certain types of applications. These need to be considered to ensure you make the right choice.

Covers

Chapter Seven

Introduction to Monitors

It is a fact that most PC applications do not require the use of a high-resolution monitor. Those of you building a low-end system or working to a budget can make economies here. Cash saved can be put towards something that is more important to you.

If you are looking to make savings wherever possible, you can buy monitors that come with integrated speakers. They won't be of good quality, but will, nevertheless, be perfectly adequate for Window's jingles, etc. Another thing to look out for is a built-in USB hub that will increase your expansion options without any extra cost.

Considering it gets more attention than any other part of a system, it is surprising just how many people pay scant regard to the monitor when purchasing their PC. Usually, the CPU, video card and RAM are of much more interest to them.

This fact is well known to manufacturers and they take advantage by tending to supply rather cheap monitors with their pre-built systems, as they do with keyboards and mice. Typically, these monitors will provide limited resolutions and refresh rates, inferior picture quality and poor power regulation.

However, it must be said that for most applications they are perfectly adequate, and for the self-builder looking to save money where possible, these low-end monitors do provide an opportunity to do this, as long as he or she is prepared to put up with their limitations.

CRT monitors are currently the most prevalent type due to their affordability, picture quality and overall performance. LCD monitors, which until fairly recently were out of most people's price range, are becoming increasingly common as the price of these devices continue to drop.

Both types have their pros and cons. When deciding between the two, you also need to consider what you will be doing on the PC, as they both have characteristics that favor certain types of applications.

Buying a Monitor

Whichever type of monitor you eventually settle for, you must first consider the following:

- Monitor dimensions
- Screen size
- Refresh rates
- Resolution
- Dot pitch

If you are fortunate enough to have ample desk space then the dimensions of the monitor probably won't be an issue. If you don't, though, then this is one good reason to go for an LCD monitor. These devices are just a few inches in depth, and will fit right back against the wall, leaving plenty of room to work.

For basic computing tasks, the size of the screen is not important, and a 15-inch CRT will be perfectly adequate for email and the like. This is an area in which economies can be made without any sacrifice in performance, as a small screen monitor will produce just as good a picture as a larger one. Whichever size you choose, just be sure it will be big enough for your needs, both now and in the future.

A monitor's refresh rate is the number of times per second that the picture is drawn on the screen. A low refresh rate will result in screen flicker that can cause headaches and put strain on the eyes. Refresh rates are affected by the screen resolution (see below). The higher the resolution, the lower the refresh rate the monitor will be able to handle.

Resolution refers to the number of individual dots of color in the display, which are known as pixels. For example, a resolution of 1074 x 768 will have 1074 pixels on the horizontal axis (picture width) and 768 on the vertical axis (picture depth). The higher the resolution, the smaller and more detailed the picture will be, and vice versa.

Dot pitch is the gap between the individual pixels and indicates the sharpness and color clarity of a monitor's display. It is measured in millimeters, and the smaller the number, the better the picture.

CRT Monitors

If you run applications that require you to switch resolutions, then a CRT monitor will be for you.

This issue of screen resolution is one of the biggest drawbacks of LCD monitors, as they only provide a good picture at one fixed resolution.

If you need a higher than normal resolution, i.e. 1600 x 1200, and above, then you will need to buy a larger monitor. This applies to both types. In the case of CRT monitors, you will be looking at 19- and 21-inch models.

The most important specification regarding picture quality is the dot pitch rating. The lower this figure the better, and high-end monitors will have a dot pitch of around 0.21 mm.

CRT monitors come in two types – Shadow Mask and Aperture Grille. Aperture Grille monitors are more expensive, but provide a better picture due to superior beam filtering technology.

Despite the inexorable march of LCD, for many people, CRT is still the monitor type of choice. One of the main reasons for this is the fact that CRT monitors provide different resolutions.

Image reprinted with permission from ViewSonic Corporation

This allows the display to be tailored to suit the user's requirements. For example, people with poor eyesight can use a low-resolution that increases the size of the display making it easier to see. Power-users and gamers, on the other hand, can set the resolution to high, enabling them to see finer detail or increase the screen "real estate", allowing more windows to be open at the same time.

The drawback is that high resolutions require refresh rates that smaller CRT monitors cannot support, resulting in screen flicker. The only way to overcome this is to buy a larger monitor – a 21-inch model should be able to provide a refresh rate of 85 Hz (which is ideal) at a resolution of 1600 x 1200 – more than adequate for the average home user. 19-inch models will only offer a refresh rate of 75 Hz (borderline) at this resolution, and 17-inch models will, typically, offer a maximum resolution of 1280 x 1024 with a refresh rate of about 65 Hz (noticeable flicker).

Therefore, if you need the fine level of detail, or large screen area that high resolutions provide, you are going to need a large desk to accommodate a bulky and more expensive 19- or 21-inch monitor.

To ensure your chosen monitor will deliver a crisp high-quality picture, you need to look at its dot pitch rating in the specifications. Top quality monitors will have a dot pitch of 0.21 or 0.22 mm, with low-end devices coming in at 0.27 or 0.28. The lower the figure, the better the picture quality. As a guide, 0.26 mm will give a reasonable picture and is the highest dot pitch you should settle for.

LCD Monitors

LCD monitors are beginning to rival their CRT counterparts on the market and many manufacturers are now supplying them as part of their pre-built systems.

These devices have several advantages over CRT monitors, and these are as follows:

Size – LCDs are physically much smaller in terms of depth, which frees up desk space for the user. Typically, they will be about three inches deep compared to some seventeen inches with a CRT.

Brightness – LCDs have a much higher level of inherent brightness. This makes them much easier to view in natural lighting conditions.

Power consumption – LCDs have very low power requirements, drawing about a third as much as a CRT. This makes them ideal for use in places such as busy stock exchanges. Because of their low power requirements, they also produce much less heat.

Radiation emission – one of the concerns with CRT monitors is the level of low-frequency radiation they emit, which some people consider harmful. This is not an issue with LCD monitors as the technology used with these devices virtually eliminates radiation emission.

Clarity – LCD monitors provide a very sharp picture that makes them ideally suited to office and still-image applications (assuming extremely high resolutions are not required).

Viewing options – many LCD monitors can be pivoted, i.e. landscape to portrait mode and vice versa. This can be useful in graphic applications.

However, LCD monitors do have some serious limitations.

Resolution – because an LCD uses a matrix of pixels to display its image, it can only have a single fixed (maximum) resolution at which the display will be optimal. Although other resolutions are available, these are achieved by interpolation techniques similar to those used by scanner manufacturers, and the results are less than satisfactory. When buying an LCD monitor you must make sure that its maximum resolution will be suitable for the type of applications you intend to use.

15-inch monitors will have a maximum resolution of 1024 x 768, 17- and 19-inch monitors 1280 x 1024, and 20-inch monitors 1600 x 1200.

Response time – this is the time the screen takes to update pixel colors. This is a very important consideration for gamers and those who want to watch movies on the PC, as an inadequate response time will result in a ghosting and streaking effect, which detracts considerably from the quality of the display. To avoid ghosting completely, look for a response time of no higher than 16 ms. NOTE: CRT monitors are not affected in this way at all.

Contrast Ratio – Contrast ratio is the ratio of light intensity between the brightest white and the darkest black that can be produced. An LCD's contrast ratio measures the relationship between black and white and is a major factor in the quality of its display. If it is too low, the picture will appear faded and washed out, whereas a high ratio will produce a vibrant and colorful picture. The lowest contrast ratio you should accept is 350:1. High-quality LCD monitors will have ratios of up to 600:1.

Viewing angle – LCD monitors have a limited viewing angle. When you look at an LCD display from the side, you will notice a loss of screen brightness and color, which doesn't happen with CRTs. This is something else to watch out for in the specifications – look for a viewing angle of 160 degrees. Low-quality models can have viewing angles as low as 60 degrees.

CRT versus LCD – Summary

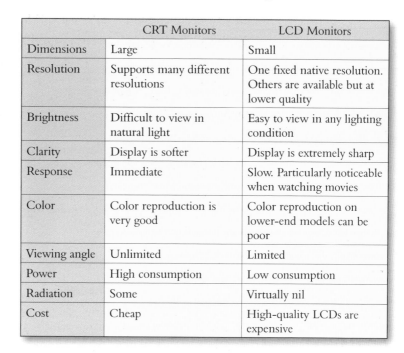

	CRT Monitors	LCD Monitors
Dimensions	Large	Small
Resolution	Supports many different resolutions	One fixed native resolution. Others are available but at lower quality
Brightness	Difficult to view in natural light	Easy to view in any lighting condition
Clarity	Display is softer	Display is extremely sharp
Response	Immediate	Slow. Particularly noticeable when watching movies
Color	Color reproduction is very good	Color reproduction on lower-end models can be poor
Viewing angle	Unlimited	Limited
Power	High consumption	Low consumption
Radiation	Some	Virtually nil
Cost	Cheap	High-quality LCDs are expensive

If you are tempted by the benefits offered by LCD monitors, don't forget they have drawbacks as well. Weigh up the pros and cons discussed in this chapter before making a decision.

LCD monitors are here to stay, and as the technology behind them continues to develop, the day when they begin to surpass CRT in terms of picture quality and overall performance is not too far away. However, that day has not yet arrived, and so, for the time being at least, CRT is best for overall performance and flexibility.

The price of many LCD monitors is now similar to their CRT equivalents and this is tempting many people to buy them, given the advantages they offer. It must be pointed out, however, that these are low-end models and they have some serious drawbacks as we have seen on the previous page.

LCD monitor technology is advancing quickly though, and these issues have largely been resolved by the manufacturers, with the result that there are models now available that do match CRTs in terms of performance. The problem, however, is the price; LCD monitors that offer the same level of all round performance as CRT monitors are considerably more expensive.

If you have a particular need for any of the advantages offered by LCD monitors, such as their smaller dimensions, and can either afford a top-end model, or are prepared to accept the limitations of lower-end models, by all means get one.

Otherwise, the advice is to stick with CRT monitors until the price of current top-end LCD monitors comes down to a more affordable level.

Installing a Monitor

All you need to do here is put it on the desk where you want it to sit, and then connect it to the AC supply and the video system.

For easy identification, VGA connections are color-coded blue.

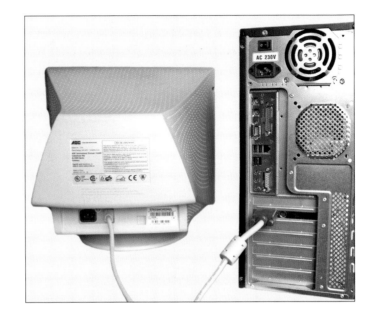

If your monitor is an LCD with a DVI input, and the video card has a DVI output, these are the ports to use.

If you are using a video card, the monitor connects to the card's VGA or DVI output. In this example, it is connected to the VGA socket. Integrated video systems will require a connection to the mainboard's VGA output.

Testing the Basic System

At this stage of proceedings, the guts of your new computer are in place. Hopefully, you haven't made any mistakes so far. If you have, they will need rectifying before you proceed any further. This chapter shows you the likely problems and how to resolve them.

Covers

Chapter Eight

Why Are We Doing This Now?

If your mainboard has an integrated video system, you can use this and leave the video card out for the time being. This will be one less potential cause of problems at this stage. Once the basic system is operational, you can then install the video card and run the test again. If it fails, you'll know immediately that the video card is the source of the problem.

At the moment, your system consists of the power supply unit, mainboard, CPU, memory and video card (as shown below). This is the bare minimum required to get a display on the monitor. However, before you go any further you also need to connect the keyboard to the system (without it the PC will refuse to boot). See page 124 for how to do this.

Without a keyboard connected to the system, the computer will not boot-up.

Having connected the keyboard, if you now test the system and it fails to work, then you know the problem lies with one of the above devices.

Don't be tempted to install everything in one go and hope it all works. Unless you've built computers before, this is not the way to do it. Test each device as you install it and then move on to the next one.

You can, of course, take the optimistic approach, and build the system completely by installing all the other parts, such as the hard drive, removable disk drives, and peripherals as well. If it works, fine. However, if it does not, you will then be faced with many more potential causes for the failure. For example, a hard drive that hasn't been configured correctly can prevent the computer from booting.

To keep head-scratching to the minimum, you should test each device as you install it and make sure it works before moving on to the next one. There is nothing wrong with optimism, but a more pragmatic approach may well save you time in the end.

Check the Monitor

Before the monitor will display a test screen, it must be isolated from the computer.

If you are in any doubt about a monitor, another way to test it is by connecting it to a different system.

If you cannot get anything on the monitor, check that the contrast and brightness controls haven't been turned right down inadvertently.

It really would be a complete waste of time to troubleshoot a system that seemingly refuses to boot-up, when all along the problem is a malfunctioning or incorrectly adjusted monitor.

Therefore, this is the stage at which you check this device. To help you do it, virtually all monitors will display a message or splash screen of some sort when switched on to indicate they are operational. For this to work, however, the monitor must be isolated from the computer, i.e. the signal cable must be disconnected from the video system's output socket.

Check it out as follows:

Plug the monitor into the wall socket. Switch it on, give it a few seconds to warm up, and then you should see a test signal similar to the one below.

No signal input
or
Cable disconnected

Monitors carry high voltages that can be lethal. These voltages will remain until discharged. Never open up a monitor for any reason.

If you don't see a test signal and the monitor lights are off, then either the monitor itself is faulty or it is not getting any power. Check the power supply, plug, cable and connections. If these are OK then the monitor must be faulty.

If you do see a light on the monitor, make sure it's not simply in Standby mode. Press the "On" switch again.

When you do have a working monitor, hook it up to the system as shown on page 94.

Check the Connections

Before you switch your system on for the first time, it may be as well to check all the connections. It is not encouraging to be greeted by a blank screen at the first attempt.

Do not forget about the power on/off switch at the rear of the power supply unit. Many people never look at the rear of the case and have no idea there is even one there.

A blank screen is not what you want to see when you first switch on

So, check the following:

One of the most likely things to get wrong is the computer's on/off button connection to the mainboard (see page 74). This will be in a row of 2-pin connectors and it is very easy to pick the wrong one.

- The PC is plugged into the wall socket.

- The switch at the rear of the power supply unit is on.

- The monitor is plugged into the wall socket.

- The monitor signal cable is connected to the video system.

- The PC's on/off switch is connected to the correct terminals on the mainboard.

- The mainboard is connected to the power supply unit.

- The CPU locking lever is pushed right down.

- The RAM modules are seated in their sockets and held in place by the clips.

- The CPU fan is connected to the mainboard.

Switch On and See What Happens

Go on then, hit the switch. If all has gone to plan so far, you'll see something like the following:

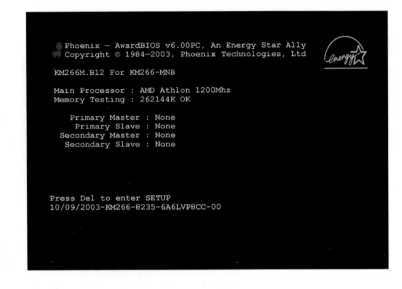

Phoenix — AwardBIOS v6.00PC, An Energy Star Ally
Copyright © 1984–2003, Phoenix Technologies, Ltd

KM266M.B12 For KM266-MNB

Main Processor : AMD Athlon 1200Mhz
Memory Testing : 262144K OK

```
     Primary Master : None
      Primary Slave : None
   Secondary Master : None
    Secondary Slave : None




Press Del to enter SETUP
10/09/2003-KM266-8235-6A6LVP8CC-00
```

As the computer boots-up you should hear a single beep. This is one of a series of beep codes (see pages 101 – 102), and in this case indicates that all is well.

The above boot screen indicates that all is well.

First, you will see details of the system's BIOS, i.e. the manufacturer and model number.

This is followed by the mainboard model.

Then the central processing unit details are displayed – manufacturer, model and clock speed.

Next is the memory test, which shows the amount of installed RAM – 256 MB, in the example above.

Finally, the fact that you can see text on the screen indicates that the video system is working as well.

Because there is no floppy drive installed at this stage, you may get a floppy drive stop error that halts the boot procedure. To override this, hit the F1 key (or the key specified on your boot screen).

The next boot screen will then open, as shown below:

Boot screens load so quickly that it can be difficult to get any information from them. However, you can stop them by pressing the Pause key on the keyboard. To resume, press Enter.

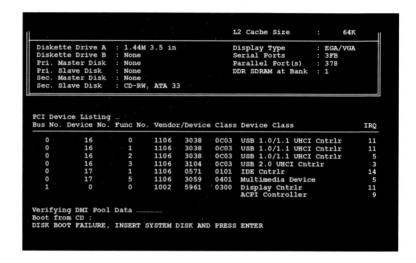

Don't worry about the disk boot error message. You are seeing this because the next stage of the boot procedure is the loading of the operating system, and as we do not yet have a hard drive installed, the BIOS cannot find one. (a boot disk is a drive that contains an operating system or associated data).

At this point the boot procedure will stop with a "DISK BOOT FAILURE" error message. This indicates that an operating system has not been found by the BIOS, and in this case, it is because the boot disk (hard drive) has not yet been installed.

If the system gets as far as this, then it is working and you can skip the rest of this chapter. If, however, it does not, then go on to the next page.

The PC Doesn't Boot

Things have not gone as planned. The PC either doesn't boot at all or doesn't reach the "Disk Boot Failure" error message. Troubleshoot as follows:

The System is Dead

First, make sure it really is "dead". Check that none of the LEDs on the case are lit, the PSU/CPU fans are not running and that the PC is not making any beeping sounds.

Absolutely the first thing to check when your PC appears to be "dead" is the power supply. Don't forget to check the external AC power supply as well.

If there are absolutely no signs of life, then you have a power supply fault. Check the following:

- Is there power at the wall socket? Plug another appliance into it, if that works then the socket is OK.

- Is the PC's power cable OK? Try substituting it with your electric kettle cable; these are often the same type.

The easiest way to establish that your power supply unit is operational is to check that the fan is working, and that the system case lights are on.

- Check that the PSU on/off switch at the top-rear of the system case is not in the off position.

If none of these is causing the problem then the power supply unit is defective and will need replacing.

The System is Alive but the Screen is Blank

The system is powered up but there is nothing on the screen.

Computer power cables are often the same as the type used with electric kettles and some other household appliances. This makes it a simple task to check them by substitution. While a fault with one of these is extremely unlikely, you have to check all the possibilities.

A faulty or incorrectly installed mainboard, CPU, RAM module or video card, can all be the cause of a blank display. Fortunately, when the BIOS chip finds a major part that is not working, it advises the user accordingly in the form of a series of coded beeps, known, not surprisingly, as beep codes. NOTE: a single beep is normal and indicates that the BIOS has found no problems. You will hear this every time at start-up.

The various BIOS chip manufacturers (Award, AMI and Phoenix), all have their own versions of these codes so you will first need to establish who is the maker of your BIOS chip. This information will be found in the mainboard manual. It might also be stamped on the chip itself.

Having done this, find the code you are hearing in the table below. This will isolate the faulty component.

The BIOS chip has an integrated diagnostic utility that alerts you to any problems it encounters during boot-up. It does this in two ways – a series of coded beeps if the problem occurs before the video system has initialized, or a text error message if the fault comes after.

No beeps at all, assuming the PC has power and the case speaker is correctly connected, is a certain indicator of a mainboard failure.

Beeps	Fault
AWARD BIOS	
1 long, 2 short	Video system
Any other sequence	Memory
AMI BIOS	
2 to 3	Memory
4	Mainboard
5	CPU
6	Mainboard
7	CPU
8	Video system
9 to 11	Mainboard
PHOENIX BIOS	
1-1-2	CPU
1-1-3	Mainboard
1-1-4	Mainboard
1-2-1 to 1-2-3	Mainboard
1-3-1	Mainboard
1-3-3 to 1-3-4	Mainboard
1-4-1	Mainboard
1-4-2	Memory
3-2-4	Mainboard
3-3-4	Video system
4-2-1 to 4-2-3	Mainboard
4-3-1 to 4-3-4	Mainboard

There is also the possibility of not hearing any beeps at all. In this case, make sure the case speaker is connected to the correct mainboard terminals. If there are still no beeps, then you have a problem with the mainboard.

Mainboard Problems

If the beep codes (or lack of) indicate a problem with the mainboard, about the only thing you can do is to try re-seating the CPU in its socket. Do the same with the RAM modules even if the beep code is not specific to memory. If the problem persists, you will have to replace the mainboard.

Fortunately, this scenario is extremely unlikely, assuming you have taken care when installing the board, and not damaged it.

Video System Problems

If you have installed a video card, this is a much more likely cause of problems.

Reseat the card in its socket and make sure it is pushed home completely.

Also, check that the video-out (VGA) cable is connected to the card's VGA socket and not the integrated mainboard video system (if this is the problem you will hear the PC beep once when switched on).

If you still have no joy, there is one more option open to you, assuming your mainboard has an integrated video system.

Switch the computer off and remove the video card from the system. Then connect the video cable to the integrated system's output. Switch on, and if you now have video, then the video card is faulty. It is very unlikely it will have been supplied in this state though; it is far more likely that you will have damaged it yourself by careless handling.

Assuming you do have a faulty circuit board, is it possible to repair it? The answer to this is yes, but it really isn't a practical option. Even if you could find someone with the expertise and requisite equipment, it would probably cost more than the board itself did. The only realistic option is to replace the board with another one.

Before condemning a mainboard, it is always worth checking that the CPU and RAM modules are firmly seated in their respective sockets.

If you are having video card problems, try removing the video card and connecting the video cable to the mainboard's integrated video system. If you now get text on the screen, then the video card is faulty and will need replacing.

Memory Problems

If the beep code indicates a memory problem, the first thing to do is make sure the RAM module is fitted correctly, as described on pages 43 and 44.

If you have an AWARD BIOS in your system, a long or continuous sequence of beeps indicates a problem with the memory.
An AMI BIOS will beep two or three times.

If the problem persists then the module is damaged and will need replacing. If you have installed two RAM modules, try removing one of them and restarting. If the PC still doesn't work, try it with the other one. While it is unlikely, if one of the modules is damaged, it could prevent the other one from working.

Otherwise, replace the module with a new one as you have almost certainly damaged it by careless handling.

Boot-up Doesn't Complete

By this we mean the PC starts but the boot procedure doesn't reach the "Disk Boot Failure" stop error message, which is as far as it can go without a hard drive installed. However, you will at least be seeing text on the screen, which indicates the mainboard, CPU and video system are all operational. This leaves only the memory as a potential cause of the problem, and in all likelihood, boot-up will stop at the memory test stage, as shown below.

If the computer starts to boot and then stops at the memory test, the RAM module is either not connected correctly or is faulty.

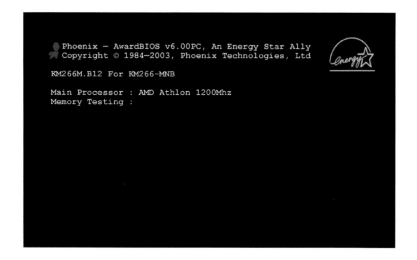

Troubleshoot as described above.

Hard Drives

One of the most confusing aspects of buying a hard drive is making sense of the various interfaces – IDE, EIDE, ATA, SATA, SCSI, etc. What do they mean and which one will be the best for you?

You also need to make sure you buy a quality drive – this is an extremely important part of the system. How do you pick the aces from the jokers though? What do drive specifications mean and which ones do you need to consider?

This chapter answers all these questions for you.

Covers

Chapter Nine

Hard Drive Introduction

The hard drive is where all your data is stored, so if it fails – and when they do, it is almost always terminal – all that data is lost.

Bear in mind, also, that these are mechanical devices, and so the one thing you can be certain about is that they will fail eventually.

These two facts make it absolutely critical that you get the best quality hard drive you can afford. This is not a component to cut costs on. Don't even think about budget or second-hand models.

The hard drive is a mechanical device.. This means it is guaranteed to fail eventually. For this reason, you must get the best quality drive you can afford. You are well advised to spend your money on a low-capacity drive of high quality, rather than one with a huge capacity, which in all likelihood you will never use.

Most current hard drives employ a technology known as S.M.A.R.T (Self Monitoring, Analysis and Reporting Technology).

S.M.A.R.T enables a drive's components to be constantly monitored for signs of impending failure, in which case an alert is flashed to the user. This gives the user time to save any important data to a different medium. The actual monitoring is carried out by the BIOS and is disabled by default.

The S.M.A.R.T system can detect around 70% of all hard drive errors.

This is a feature well worth having, so make sure that the drive you buy supports it.

When buying a hard drive you need to consider the following:

- Interface – USB, Firewire, ATA or SCSI
- External or internal models
- Storage capacity
- Specifications
- Latest technology
- Configurations

Hard Drive Interfaces

Don't be confused by references to IDE, EIDE, ATA, DMA and UDMA when looking at hard drive specifications. Essentially, they all mean the same thing – the drive in question uses the ATA interface.

Advanced Drive Electronics (ATA)

The ATA interface can be a perplexing topic as it has several different names and versions, all of which essentially indicate the same thing. Much confusion is caused by the fact that it is often referred to as EIDE (Enhanced Integrated Drive Electronics). This is a misnomer, though, as EIDE actually refers to a device that has an integrated controller, rather than on the mainboard as used to be the norm. When you see a drive described as EIDE, it really means the device operates on the ATA interface.

You will also see ATA hard drives advertised as DMA and UDMA. These abbreviations stand for Direct Mode Access and Ultra Direct Mode Access, respectively. These are improved versions of the ATA interface that allow data transfer to and from the hard drive to take place with minimal input from the CPU.

If you want to buy a mainboard with the SATA interface to keep abreast of current technology, but have a perfectly good ATA hard drive that you want to use, you need to invest in a SATA adapter that will convert the SATA controller to work with your ATA hard drive.

However, you will lose the 150 MB/s bandwidth of the SATA interface.

The ATA interface also has different speeds, i.e. data transfer rates. Currently, the two most common are 100 MB/s and 133 MB/s.

Serial ATA (SATA)

The latest evolution of ATA is known as SATA (Serial ATA). This new interface uses a slimline cable (shown below), as opposed to the 80-conductor flat ribbon cables used by ATA drives. It also has a new type of power connector.

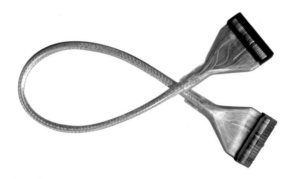

Another advantage offered by the SATA interface is the much smaller slimline cables used. These are much easier to manipulate within the confines of the system case than the traditional ribbon cables. They also offer much less resistance to air circulation.

SATA offers increased transfer rates of 150 MB/s, longer cable lengths (about one meter), lower power consumption and reduced electromagnetic interference. Future generations projected for 2005 and 2007 will increase the bandwidth to 300 MB/s and 600 MB/s, respectively.

Small Computer System Interface (SCSI)

SCSI is completely different to ATA. It is actually a system interface as it is not just limited to disk drives.

SCSI requires the use of a host adapter. This can be integrated on the mainboard or may be purchased as a PCI card that plugs into the mainboard. Whichever, it provides a system BUS that can

handle up to seven separate devices. These can be hard drives, tape drives, CD-ROM drives, scanners, etc.

The main advantages of SCSI are speed, performance and reliability. SCSI drives operate much faster than ATA drives, with data transfer rates up to 320 MB/s. While the next generation of SATA hard drives will close the gap in speed, they will still be a mile away from SCSI in terms of performance and reliability.

Although PC manufacturers are now fitting SATA hard drives in their desktop PCs, SCSI hard drives are, and will remain, the choice for servers, corporate and power-users, despite the fact that they cost four times as much as ATA equivalents.

Firewire

Firewire is a high-speed BUS interface originally designed by Apple and offers data transfer rates of up to 800 MB/s.

Other advantages are the ability to run up to 63 devices, no need for CPU intervention, plug-and-play support, hot-swapping support, a slim 6-wire cable, and the supply of up to 45 watts of power per port, allowing most devices to operate without a separate power supply.

Firewire drives are ideal for applications that require seriously high data transmission speeds.

Firewire hard drives are mainly external devices and have to be connected to a Firewire port. If the mainboard is not Firewire-compatible, and few are, then a Firewire PCI card needs to be installed. This will supply up to four ports.

Despite the many advantages, Firewire drives have never really caught on with desktop PCs, due mainly to their high price.

However, for all that, Firewire is the fastest interface around at the moment, and it is particularly useful in high-speed multimedia applications, such as realtime audio and video-editing, where fast data transmission is required.

Universal Serial Bus (USB)

USB2 is some forty-times faster than USB1. So if you decide on a USB hard drive, get one that supports USB2.

USB is a computer interface that is very similar in concept to Firewire. It will allow up to 127 devices to run simultaneously on a computer and has many of the features offered by Firewire, such as hot-swapping, plug-and-play and power provision.

USB comes in two versions – USB1, which has a maximum data transfer speed of 12 MB/s, and the much faster USB2, which has a transfer rate of 480 MB/s.

USB2 is now the USB standard and will be found on virtually all mainboards built from 2004 onwards. While not as fast as Firewire, it is considerably faster than the ATA and SATA interfaces.

If you decide to opt for a USB hard drive, you will be restricted to an external model. This will cost a lot more than an internal IDE drive of similar capacity.

NOTE: USB can only be used with external devices.

The following table summarizes the pros & cons of the interfaces we have discussed, with cost based on an 80 GB hard drive. Prices are approximate and for the purpose of comparison only.

Interface	Speed	Cost	Comments
ATA	133	$60	Cheap, on the way out
SATA	150	$80	Latest ATA version
USB2	480	$110	Fast, external devices only
Firewire	800	$135	Fastest, external devices only
SCSI	320	$260	Costly, best for performance

Internal or External?

External hard drives offer many advantages over internal models – faster data transmission, ease of installation and portability between PCs.

While you will probably buy an internal hard drive (which is what most people do), there is always the option of going for an external model.

USB External hard drive from Western Digital

Because the dimensions of external hard drives are not limited, as they are for internal models, these devices are available with much greater storage capacities – 500 GB models are available, as opposed to about 250 GB for internal models.

As ever though, there are pros and cons involved here.

The pros include ease of installation – simply connect it to the USB or Firewire port and follow the onscreen instructions.

Data is easily transferable – unplug the drive from one PC and plug it into another. This is much simpler than removing an internal drive from the case, installing it in another, and then setting it up in the BIOS.

As they work via USB or Firewire, data transfer is much faster than with an internal ATA hard drive.

External hard drives need a more robust case, and also a separate power supply. This makes them expensive devices.

Less parts inside the system case adds up to less heat being generated – the cooler the system, the more stable it will be.

The only real disadvantage is the expense – external hard drives cost considerably more, typically two to three times as much as an internal model, as they usually need a separate power supply, not to mention a sturdy case. In addition, of course, you have to find somewhere to put it. At least an internal drive is tucked away out of sight.

Hard Drive Configurations

RAID configurations allow you to setup a combination of drives in different ways, each of which provides specific benefits. However, in most cases (see margin note below) this will require a RAID-enabled mainboard or a PCI RAID controller.

Very few people ever install two hard drives in their system, and those who do will usually set them up in a master/slave relationship – see page 114.

However, there are alternatives to this and these come in the form of RAID (Redundant Array of Independent Disks). RAID is a way of configuring a combination of hard drives to gain specific benefits. Traditionally, RAID has been found in server and corporate environments where the need for the advantages it gives is greater. However, the introduction of low-cost RAID controllers has made it a viable option for the home-user.

Of the various RAID configurations, two, possibly three, may be of interest in a home-PC environment.

If you are running Windows 2000 or Windows XP Professional, it is possible to have a software RAID setup. This is controlled by the operating system. The advantage is cost – no RAID controller to buy and ease of setting-up.

There are, however, disadvantages. Software setups do have an adverse effect on general system performance, and are not as efficient or reliable as hardware setups.

RAID 0 is the simplest type and requires at least two, preferably identical, hard drives, and a RAID controller as shown below.

With a RAID 0 setup, data being transferred is split up (striped) equally between the drives, which work in parallel. If two drives

are being used, each one handles half the file with the result that data transfer speed is doubled. The more hard drives you have, the greater the increase in performance. This is an ideal way of taking two or more, cheap, low-performance drives, and turning them into one high-performance unit.

RAID 1 mirrors the data, i.e. writes a separate copy on each drive. The advantage of this is data protection – if one drive fails, the data can be recovered from one of the other drives.

RAID 0+1 is a combination of RAID 0 and 1 and gives the advantages of both. However, it requires at least four drives in order to do it.

Buying a Hard Drive

Modern hard drives provide a tremendous amount of storage capacity – external models up to 500 GB and internal models up to 250 GB.

However, when you consider that Windows XP will use about 1.5 GB, and relatively few applications will use more than 100 MB, all this storage capacity really is quite unnecessary. For typical home-users, 40 – 60 GB may be enough. The only time anyone is likely to need higher capacity is when the PC is used to store large amounts of high-resolution video, such as movies.

Remember, every GB of capacity will cost you money. If you are never likely to use it, what is the point of buying it? You would be better off spending the money on extra RAM.

If you use seventy percent or more of a hard drive's capacity, its performance will start dropping off. Bear this in mind when making your decision regarding the capacity you are likely to need.

Storage Capacity

Having decided on what type of drive you want – internal or external, and the desired interface – you now need to turn your attention to the desired storage capacity.

This is not easy, so try to be a bit scientific about it. As every GB costs money, you don't want to be buying more than you are ever likely to use. Nor, however, do you want to find yourself running short. Take a look at your present system, see how many GBs you have used, and then add on whatever you think you are likely to need in the future. When doing this, bear in mind that each successive version of virtually all major software titles are larger than the ones that preceded them. Remember, also, that video and graphics eat up hard drive space at an enormous rate.

When you've arrived at a figure, add thirty percent to it. The reason for doing this is that hard drives only perform efficiently at up to seventy percent of their capacity. Any higher than this and data transfer rates start slowing down.

The only way to evaluate the quality of a hard drive is to study its specifications. The most important of these are the type of interface used, Rotational Speed and Access Time. Storage capacity is not an indicator.

Do not confuse Access Time with Seek Time, another specification often listed in spec sheets; they are not the same. Seek Time is a measure of the speed at which the drive can position its read/write heads over any particular data track. Access Time is the sum total of Seek Time and Latency.

Latency is the time between the read/write head stopping over the data track and the first byte of the data appearing under the head.

All hard drives have the latencies shown below:

5400 rpm drives – 5.56 ms

7200 rpm drives – 4.17 ms

10,000 rpm drives – 3.0 ms

15,000 rpm drives – 2.0 ms

If you want to know the Access Time of a particular drive and the spec sheet lists only the Seek Time, then add the relevant Latency figure to the Seek Time.

Technical Specifications

The specs listed in the table below relate to internal hard drives, and are the things you need to look out for in order to pick out the good performers.

	Low-End	Mid-Range	Top-End
	ATA	SATA	SCSI
Interface Speed (external data rate)	100/133	150	320
	The speed at which data is transferred from the drive to the system. The differences between the various versions of ATA are negligible, but there is a big difference between ATA/SATA and SCSI/Firewire/USB – SCSI particularly. Measured in MB/s. An important factor.		
Internal Data Rate	400 to 600	600 to 750	800 to 900
	This is the speed at which a drive's internal read channel can transfer data from the magnetic media. Internal Data Rates are measured in Megabits per second. More important than the Interface speed.		
Rotational Speed	5400	7200	10000 - 15000
	The speed at which a drive's platters spin directly affects the speed at which the drive reads and writes data. This is a critical performance factor, and the faster the better. Measured in rpm.		
Access Time	12	8.5	3.6
	The time needed to locate data on a drive's disk platters. This is an important indicator of a drive's performance. Measured in ms.		
Buffer Size or Cache Memory	2	2	8
	The Buffer is a memory cache on a drive where data is temporarily stored, and is measured in MB. Not critical but the larger it is, the better.		

Preparing a Drive for Installation

The hard drive must be correctly jumpered for the intended purpose, i.e. master or slave. To this end, you will find a jumper-positioning table somewhere on the body of the drive unit.

Hard drives have to be configured before they can be used – in a single-drive setup, the drive will be the master, in a two-drive setup, one will be the master and the other the slave.

To facilitate this, hard drives have a block at the rear with four pairs of pins, each pair providing a different configuration that is selected by means of a 2-pin jumper.

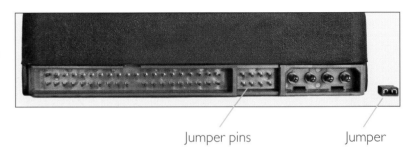

Jumper pins   Jumper

You are also likely to find three other jumper configurations. While you almost certainly won't need to use them, they are:

- *Cable Select – this is an alternative method of setting up a master/slave relationship. However, it requires the use of a special IDE cable that must be purchased separately. For this reason, cable select is rarely used in a desktop PC.*

- *32 GB capacity limit – this setting limits the drive's capacity to 32 GB, and was introduced as a work-around for older systems that had trouble recognizing drives larger than 32 GB. With modern systems, this is no longer an issue.*

- *Master with a non-ATA compatible slave – if you use a non-ATA compatible drive as the slave, the system might not recognize the master drive. This setting fixes the problem.*

Most drives are supplied with the jumper set to the master position, and if you are intending to just install one drive, all you need do is check that the jumper is in the correct position. This can be done by means of the jumper/pin table, which you will find on the drive case, as shown below.

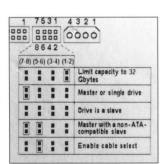

However, if you going to install two drives, then you must choose the one you want as the master (the better or newer of the two), and place the jumpers on both accordingly.

Once this has been done, you are ready to install the drives.

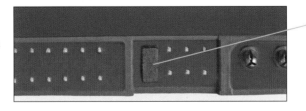

Drive set up as the Master

Installing a Hard Drive

At the front of the system case you will find various bays in which to install your drives.

A computer case has two bay compartments — 3.5 inch for hard and floppy drives, and 5.25 inch for CD and DVD drives.

Low-quality cases might not have supporting shelves that aid installation. In this event, you will have to support the drive with one hand and insert the screws with the other — not so easy.

You might also encounter sharp edges in this type of case.

CD and DVD drive bays

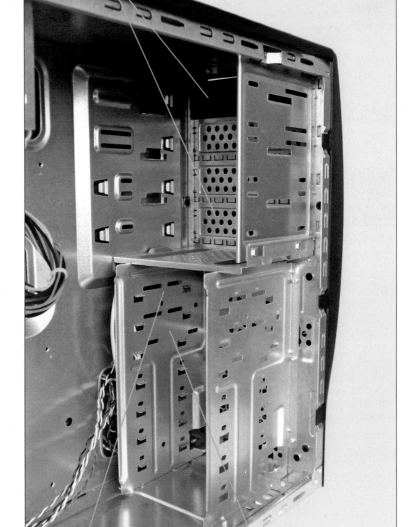

Floppy drive bay

Hard drive bays

1 Select the second bay from the top (the first one is for the floppy drive) and slide the hard drive in along the supporting shelves.

Make sure you fit the drive unit the right way up. It won't last long if you use it upside down. The 4-pin power socket should be on the right.

Secure the drive with screws at both sides. To get at the left-hand side you may need to remove the side panel. Don't be tempted to ignore this step – the drive must be held absolutely rigid.

2 Line up the drive's screw holes with the slots in the bay assembly and secure the drive with the supplied screws.

If you decide to fit more than one hard drive, do not stack them too closely. This could well cause them to overheat. Leave a space between them.

The mainboard has two main IDE channels, the Primary and Secondary, plus another one for the floppy drive.

You must install your hard drive on the Primary channel. This will be identified by the colored socket on the mainboard. The Secondary channel socket will be black.

3 Now you need to connect the drive to the mainboard. Take the IDE ribbon cable and plug the colored end (colors used vary) into the corresponding IDE socket on the mainboard.

The drive's IDE cable will have three connectors – a colored one (usually blue or red) that connects to the mainboard, a black one at the other end that connects to the drive, and a gray one in the middle. This last is the one you would use to connect a second hard drive as a slave.

4 The other end, which will be black, plugs into the back of the drive.

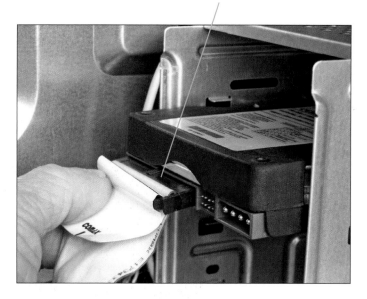

You will find that the IDE cable connector and socket are keyed to make it impossible to fit them incorrectly. If the connector won't go one way, turn it over and try again. Take some care when doing this – it is very easy to bend, or even break, the drive's pins.

5 Finally, hook up the drive's power supply.

IDE ribbon cables are unwieldy affairs, and are usually much longer than they need to be. Rather than leaving them draped untidily all over the place, fold up the slack parts of the cable and secure them with an elastic band as shown below.

Keep the inside of the case as free of obstructions as possible. This will aid good air circulation, which is essential to keep your components cool. Keeping your IDE cables as short as possible by folding them up, will help to achieve this.

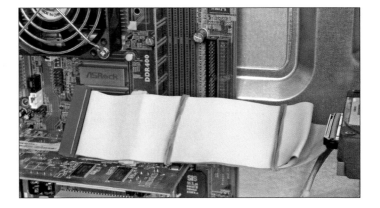

Then tuck them out of the way as far as possible. Not only will this make your work look neater and more professional, it will also help to maintain a good circulation of air inside the case.

Input Devices

The input devices covered in this chapter are the mouse and keyboard. You are probably already thinking "Well, what's there to say about these? They all do the same thing; in fact they even look the same."

The next few pages will show you that there are, in fact, many different types of mouse and keyboard, some of which are designed for specific applications.

Covers

Chapter Ten

Types of Keyboard

Most people find the basic models commonly supplied with pre-built systems to be perfectly adequate, and for self-builders on a budget, this will also be the case.

Program-specific Keyboards

However, for those with a bit more cash available, the buying options are much increased. For example, you can buy keyboards designed for use with specific applications such as the Internet and Microsoft Office. Other keyboards of this type are more general, and provide keys for a range of applications. A good example from Viewsonic is shown below:

Word, Excel & Powerpoint keys

Internet keys such as Back & Forward

Multimedia keys such as Play & Stop

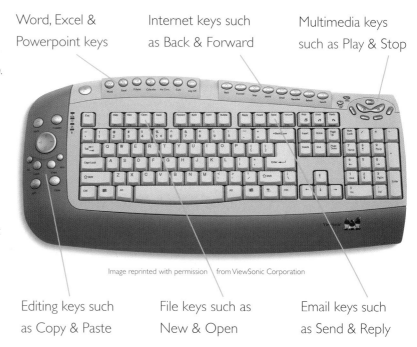

Image reprinted with permission from ViewSonic Corporation

Editing keys such as Copy & Paste

File keys such as New & Open

Email keys such as Send & Reply

Cordless Keyboards

These are becoming increasingly popular as they reduce the amount of clutter on the desktop. They also allow the user to sit a lot further back from the monitor, thus reducing eye-strain and exposure to any electromagnetic radiation emitted by the monitor.

These keyboards are very expensive though, and cost five or six times as much as a standard keyboard.

While some types of game can be played almost entirely with a joystick or gamepad, others rely much more on the keyboard. Certain movements like jumping and kicking out simultaneously, such as you will find in a martial arts game, require several keys to be pressed at the same time.

Standard keyboards will only react to two or three simultaneous keys – anything else is ignored. A good gaming keyboard, however, will allow four to six keys. In fact, some will allow an unlimited amount.

Gaming Keyboards

Gamers are well catered for in the keyboard stakes with a range of models available, all designed to enhance the gaming experience, particularly online gaming. A typical example, the Saitek PC Gamers Keyboard, is shown below.

You can also find keyboards tailored for specific games. Take a look at Ideazon's website at www.zboard.com. Here you will find a range of keyboards designed for use with games such as Doom 3, Medal of Honor and EverQuest 2.

Ideazon's Z-Board features a base unit that can be customized with swappable keysets, such as the Doom 3 keyset shown opposite.

Doom 3 keyboard from Ideazon

Those of you always on the move might like to take their keyboard with them. This is easy with a roll-up keyboard. Made of a thin pliant material such as silicon, you simply roll it up and stuff it in a bag. These devices are very thin and weigh only a few ounces.

In general, keyboards are the same as everything else in life – you get what you pay for. While the cheap keyboards supplied with pre-built systems may be adequate, they will never perform as well, or have features such as programmable keys, that more expensive models will have.

Types of Mouse

The only problem with standard wheel mice is the issue of requiring periodic cleaning. This is no big deal though. Simply remove the bottom plate and scrape the accumulated gunk from the wheels.

Standard Wheel Mouse

In the same way as with keyboards, low-end wheel mice are cheap and functional, but offer very little else, except maybe, a third programmable button.

A cordless mouse requires batteries and will go through them at a considerable rate (depending on how much you use it, of course). This can prove expensive after a while, so a good tip is to use rechargeable batteries. All you need is a cheap charging unit and four rechargeables – two in use and two recharging.

Top-end mice usually come with rechargeable batteries anyway. They will also have a small desktop recharging unit into which you park the mouse when you've finished working. While you are catching up on the baseball, the mouse batteries are being recharged.

Disadvantages of this type of mouse are that periodically the scroll wheels inside will need cleaning, and that they require the use of a mouse mat. Plus, of course, the cable that will be draped all over the desktop.

Cordless Mouse

Cordless mice use the same radio frequency technology as cordless keyboards, and offer the same advantage of not needing a physical connection to the PC in the form of a cable.

In all other respects though, they are the same as a wheel mouse and will need cleaning periodically.

Optical Mouse

For a few dollars more, you can buy an optical mouse, as shown below. These devices use an electronic sensor to detect movement.

A new type of mouse recently released onto the market by Logitech, is their MX™ 1000 Laser Cordless Mouse. Given its title, you won't be surprised to learn that this device uses a laser. According to Logitech, the mouse is twenty-times more sensitive to surface detail (tracking power) than its optical cousins, and can be used even on polished and reflective surfaces.

As they have no moving parts, they are essentially maintenance-free, other than changing the batteries occasionally. Apart from offering more precise control than wheel mice do, they also have the advantage of being able to be used on most surfaces – a mouse mat is not needed.

Optical mice have the big advantage of not requiring a special surface, as do wheel mice. They will work on literally any surface except glass.

Optical sensor

Trackball Mouse

From an ergonomic viewpoint, trackballs are recognized as being the easiest type to use, as little or no wrist movement is required.

Essentially, a trackball is an inverted mouse. To operate it, you rotate the ball with your thumb, fingers or palm. While they take some getting used to, they do offer several advantages. For example, as the devices are stationary, they require little room and can be used on any surface.

They can be operated with one finger and require no arm or wrist movement. This makes them ideal for those with disabilities such as arthritis. Trackballs also offer a high level of precision, which is why they are often found in graphic studios.

Mouse and Keyboard Installation

Standard Mice and Keyboards

Mice and keyboards are the simplest part of the system to install. If they use the traditional PS/2 connections, just plug them into the PS/2 sockets at the top-rear of the case, as shown below. USB devices are just as easy – plug them into a USB port.

The only thing you need to watch out for is that you connect the mouse and keyboard to the correct ports. These are identical, and right next to each other. To this end you will usually find the cables and sockets are color-coded – purple for the keyboard and green for the mouse.

Cordless Mice and Keyboards

These devices come with an additional receiving unit, which receives the signals from the device and then passes them to the computer. An example is shown below.

Some cordless devices will require the device and the receiver to be pushed up close before a connection is established. You can then tuck the receiver away out of sight.

Image reprinted with permission from ViewSonic Corporation

To install the device, you need to connect the receiver to the PC via a USB or PS/2 port. Then place the batteries in the mouse and a radio frequency connection should be made automatically. Some models, though, will require a button to be pressed on the receiver and possibly the device as well.

Sound Systems

Do you actually need a sound card in your system? Unless you have specific requirements, the answer to this is no – find out why in the following pages.

This chapter will also explain which applications do require a sound card and what to look for in the cards specifications.

Covers

Chapter Eleven

In General

Sound is one of the less important aspects of a computer, as for most tasks, it simply isn't needed. That said, there are probably very few people who would opt to do without it completely as it does add another element to computing. For gamers it is essential.

For the self-builder working to a budget, the computer's sound system offers an opportunity to cut costs. Unless there is a specific need for any of the features provided by a dedicated sound card, an integrated sound system will fit the bill nicely.

When buying a high-quality sound card for listening to music or gaming, you will also need to factor in the price for a set of high-quality speakers. These can cost as much as the card itself, and so the setup as a whole can turn out to be expensive.

For most people, the sound systems integrated into most mainboards will be more than adequate for all their sound requirements.

For those who want high quality sound reproduction, or musicians who need music-mastering facilities, the issue is more complicated, as a top-end sound card will be required. These come with bewildering sets of specifications, features and sockets, and require a bit of homework to ensure the correct choice is made.

For the self-builder who is working to a budget, the high cost of top-end sound cards also needs to be considered, as these can cost even more than video cards.

However, for most people, a computer's sound system is an area in which economies can be made with very little penalty in terms of functionality or performance.

Integrated Sound Systems

In the past, the vast majority of computers were supplied with two nasty little speakers, which were good for reproducing the operating system's clicks and jingles and little else. The integrated sound systems supplied with these PCs were equally basic.

As with integrated video, integrated sound systems have their pros and cons.

The advantages of integrated sound are:
• No cost.
• No PCI slot used.
• No hardware to be installed.

Disadvantages are:
• Slight degradation of overall system performance.
• Performance levels, while adequate, do not match those offered by sound cards.
• Limited features.
• Limited input & output sockets

Thankfully, the situation is rather different today, and many of the mainboards currently on the market come with quite sophisticated sound systems that are good enough even for the gamer. It is quite common now to find systems offering six-channel 5.1 surround sound that can take advantage of multi-speaker setups.

Integrated sound systems do not require the use of a PCI slot as do sound cards. This gives you more room for expansion in other areas.

The only drawbacks are that they rely on the PC's CPU and memory to do the hard work, thus reducing overall system performance. In addition, they provide less in the way of input and output sockets than sound cards do. This can be restrictive.

When considering an integrated sound system, look for supported technologies such as DirectSound 3D and multi-channel speaker support.

This mainboard may offer six-channel 5.1 surround sound but it does not supply all the necessary outputs. This means messing about with software settings to get all the speakers working

Also, good as they are, they still do not provide the kind of high-fidelity required by the music purist, nor do they offer anything to the musician in the way of authoring features.

If you do decide to take the integrated route, take a look at the specifications as there are still systems around which are not so good. Basically, the more features offered, the better the performance will be. Look for things such as support for DirectX, EAX, DirectSound 3D and multi-channel speaker systems.

Sound Cards

People who need to buy a dedicated sound card will fall into one of the following categories:

- Speed aficionados who don't want to sacrifice even the small hit in performance that integrated sound will make on their system.

- Musicians who need specific mastering functions such as Wave Table Synthesis support.

- Gamers who want to get the maximum sound effects from their games.

- Music buffs who require the highest possible quality of sound reproduction.

One of the best known manufacturers of sound cards is Creative Labs, who can be found at at www. creative.com.

This company manufactures a range of cards to suit all pockets. Currently, their top-end model is the "Sound Blaster Audigy 2 ZS Platinum Pro".

This card is supplied with a break-out box, and has a 108 Db signal-to-noise ratio and 24-bit audio, making it a serious piece of kit.

Gamers and music buffs will be well served by the Audigy Pro.

Budget Sound Cards

If you are looking to make your system as fast as possible, then integrated sound is out due to the demands it makes on the system's CPU and memory. While the drop in performance is relatively slight, it is, nevertheless, there.

In this situation, a low- to mid-level sound card will suffice, as all you are looking for is something to take the load off the CPU and memory. Anything else it offers is a bonus.

A card like the 5.11 from Trust (pictured above) will be more than adequate. This card offers full 5.1 surround sound, is DirectX and EAX compatible, and is very reasonably priced. Alternatives are the low-end SoundBlaster cards from Creative.

Professional Sound Cards

Those interested in creating music on their PCs, will look at professional sound cards that provide features such as balanced analog inputs/outputs, digital inputs/outputs in AES/EBU or S/PDIF formats, full duplex, and dedicated wave-mixers.

Do not overlook the "connectivity" of the sound card. The more inputs and outputs it has, the more you will be able to do with it, e.g. microphone recording, the attachment of multiple-speaker systems, digital audio devices, and other electronic equipment such as a stereo system.

When buying a professional card, look for one that includes a break-out box as shown below. This sits on the desktop and houses the input/output jacks and the audio converters.

For high-quality sound output look for a sound card that is supplied with a separate break-out box or hub.

This type of arrangement eliminates the issue of noise by converting the analog signal to digital form *before* it is sent to the card in the PC. The result is much cleaner recordings – cheaper cards have the jacks and audio converters on the card itself, where noise will be induced from nearby parts such as the hard drive.

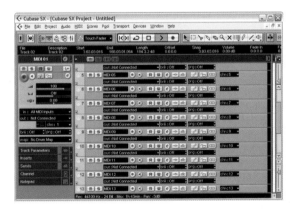

Used in conjunction with a suitable mastering application, such as Steinberg's Cubase, a professional sound card will turn a PC into a fully-fledged recording studio.

Sound Cards for Gamers

Gamers who are not satisfied with the quality of integrated sound need to look at several aspects of sound cards before buying.

DirectX support is just as important for a sound card as it is for a video card. Make sure the card supports the latest version of DirectX.

The first is multiple-speaker support. While integrated sound systems go as far as 5.1, there are 8.1 speaker systems on the market, and for these a compatible sound card will be required. Surround Sound and 3D-sound support will also be important, 3D-sound particularly. These technologies help to accurately recreate the relative positioning of sound in a three-dimensional game world, and lead to a more realistic gaming experience.

When applied to a sound card, the term "channel" has two separate meanings. These are as follows:

1) The number of speakers or headsets that can be connected to the card. A card with one output jack will be able to support two channels; each channel supporting one speaker – one left, one right. If it has two jacks, it will support four speakers, and so on.

2) The number of simultaneous sounds the card can process by itself.

With 3D-sound and a suitable set of speakers, the bullets in this game will sound as though they are whistling over your head

Also, consider the number of simultaneous sounds (channels) the sound card can handle before involving the system's CPU. A minimum figure to aim at is 32. Better cards can handle up to 128 channels. The higher the figure, the less is required of the CPU, leaving it free to run the computer smoothly.

The more APIs (application program interfaces) the card supports, the better. These allow the game to communicate with the sound card, and different types of sound use specific APIs. If they are not supported by the card, then you will be missing out on some of the game's sound effects.

The gamer might also want to look at the specs that determine the quality of the sound cards output (see page 131). While fidelity is not so important in a gaming environment as it is to someone who listens to music, the gamer might like to chill out with a nice violin concerto, having just saved the world from marauding aliens.

High-Fidelity Sound Cards

Music buffs who like to listen to crystal-clear high-fidelity audio, need to investigate a different set of specifications. 3D and Surround Sound will be less important than the purity of the sound card's output. This is indicated by the following specifications:

Another important specification that the high-fidelity lover might care to consider is the sound card's audio bit depth. In digital audio, the bit depth is a measure of the accuracy of sound reproduction. Most cards these days are 16-bit, which is good enough for most people.

There are, however, 24-bit cards on the market, and these take sound to another level in terms of clarity and detail.

- Signal-to-noise ratio (SNR) – measured in decibels, a high signal-to-noise ratio means more music and less noise, so the higher this figure, the better.

- Total harmonic distortion (THD) – this is a measure of a different type of noise (we won't go into the details here), which basically distorts the signal. THD is measured in percent and the lower the percentage, the better.

- Frequency response (FR) – this is the range of frequencies produced by a sound device and is specified in upper and lower limits. NOTE: 20 Hz to 20 KHz encompasses the full range of human hearing.

Sounds within the 20 Hz – 20 KHz range are audible to humans.

The closer to these thresholds a sound card's frequency response is, the more you will hear.

Taken as a whole, these three specifications are the measure of a sound card's output quality. The figures in the following table show what to expect from low- end, mid-range and top-end sound cards.

	Low-end	Mid-range	Top-end
SNR	75 Db	90 Db	100 Db
THD	0.5%	0.05%	0.01%
FR	20 Hz - 20 KHz	20 Hz to 20 KHz	15 Hz to 40 KHz

For real clarity, consider buying one of the sound cards that comes paired with a break-out box as described on page 129.

Finally, whatever type of sound card you buy, if you are running Windows XP, make sure you get one that comes with XP certified drivers. This will ensure that it is XP compatible. Sound cards, even good ones, are notorious for driver issues.

Installing a Sound Card

The quality of a sound card's output is affected by high-frequency interference generated by other parts in the system, such as the hard drive. Better cards include circuitry to filter out much of this interference, but even so, some will get through.

You can minimize this by installing the card as far away from other components as possible.

Outside the case, make sure the speaker cables are well away from other cables, particularly power cables.

Install the sound card as you would any other expansion card. One thing to be aware of, though, is that these cards are prone to picking up interference from other system devices. This will be heard by the user in the form of hissing, crackling or humming. However, if your card is supplied with a break-out box, this will be much less of an issue.

To minimize interference as much as possible, situate the card as far away as you can from other devices.

1 Here, we have installed the sound card in the next but one PCI slot to the video card.

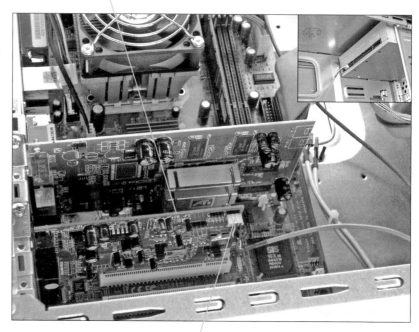

2 When you've installed the card, don't forget to connect the 4-pin analog cable coming from the CD drive (inset).

If you also have a break-out box, connect it to the card's output sockets with the supplied cables, as detailed in the instructions.

Removable Media Drives

One of the biggest boons for PC users in recent years has been the introduction of writable CD and DVD drives. Self-builders will definitely want to incorporate one of these into their new systems.

This chapter shows you what is available, explains all the various CD and DVD formats, and shows how to pick the one best suited to your needs.

There are also other types of removable media drive you may want to consider, such as Superdisk and Zip drives.

Covers

Chapter Twelve

What's Available?

The simplest way to avoid the issue of which type of drive to buy with regard to format compatibility, is to buy a multi-function drive. These are compatible with all the current CD/DVD disc formats.

Given the enormous storage capacities offered by today's removable media, no self-respecting system can possibly be without one. The uses for these discs are endless – movie and music recording, system backups, data transfer between PCs, etc. The problem is choosing the right one.

Do you settle for a basic CD writer or do you splash out for a DVD writer? If you do buy a DVD device, which format do you go for – DVD-ROM, DVD+R, DVD-R, DVD-RAM, DVD-RW or DVD+RW?

Used in conjunction with a suitable backup utility, such as Powerquest's Drive Image, high-capacity CDs/DVDs enable you to make a complete or selective backup of your system. In the event of major problems, you can restore the system in a few minutes.

Then there is the humble floppy drive. In terms of storage capacity, floppy disks offer a measly 1.44 MB, compared to 650 MB for a CD and 4.7 GB for a DVD disc. Are they worth buying at all?

Some drives, known as multi-function drives, can handle any type of disc – CD-ROM, CD-R, CD-RW and DVD. They are, however, expensive. Is it more cost effective to buy one of these or to go for separate devices?

Your choices are:

- Floppy drives
- CD-ROM drives
- CD writers
- DVD drives
- Multi-function drives

Floppy Drives

Floppy disks are ideal for the transportation of small files. Nearly everyone has a floppy disk drive in their computer.

You may well be pondering whether it's actually worth the bother of buying and installing a floppy drive in your new PC.

Superdisk drives use a disk that can hold 250 MB of data. They can also increase the storage capacity of a standard 1.44 MB floppy to 32 MB. This is done by reformatting the disk with a supplied software program. The only drawback is that floppies reformatted to 32 MB can only be read by another Superdisk drive.

Well, in our opinion, the answer is yes. While they are slow and the disks hold very little data compared to a CD, the fact remains that they are the only removable drives that are more or less guaranteed to be found on any desktop PC (there are still many computers that don't have a CD writer). Thus, they provide virtually all of us with a simple and easy means of transferring data from one PC to another.

Furthermore, a floppy disk is relatively rugged in construction compared to a CD, and is easily slipped into a top pocket.

Also, virtually all system cases come with a 3.5 inch floppy drive bay. So, given that floppy drives cost next to nothing, you may as well have one.

Another option is to buy one of the Superdisk drives. These devices use disks that have capacities up to 250 MB, although the disks themselves are more expensive than a floppy disk. The big advantage with these drives is that they are also compatible with standard 1.44 MB floppies. A further boon is that many of them have a formatting system that can increase the storage capacity of a floppy disk to a comparatively whopping 32 MB. With one of these devices, that pile of redundant floppies that most PC users have lying about will suddenly take on a new lease of life.

CD-ROM Drives

It is important to realize that not all drives with the same "X" rating offer the same level of performance. There are other factors involved, such as the quality of the control circuitry and the reading technology employed (CAV or CLV). As ever, drives that are low in price, usually offer low performance as well.

A $50 52X drive has to offer better performance than a $20 52X drive, otherwise nobody is going to buy it.

For your new computer, the very minimum you will want in terms of CD capabilities is a CD-ROM drive. These devices are read-only, which means that you can access the data on the disc but you cannot write anything to it. If you have no need for CD writing, one of these drives will be the least expensive option for your PC.

Interfaces used with these drives are the same as with hard drives (see pages 107 to 109), and the pros and cons of these apply equally.

When looking at CD-ROM drive specifications, you may also see an interface called ATAPI (ATA Packet Interface). This is an extension that enables the EIDE/ATA interface to support CD-ROM drives.

CD-ROM drives are advertised in speeds of 32X, 48X, 56X, etc. – 56X being the current standard. These figures refer to the drive's data transfer rate, so 56X is the one to go for if you want maximum performance. However, it must be said that the performance differential between 32X and 56X is not that much (the increase in noise with 56X is, though).

The CAV method of disc reading provides optimal data transfer rates. A further advantage is much less disc vibration, and hence noise. This is because the speed at which the disc rotates is constant.

CLV uses a variable rotation speed that increases as the laser moves towards the inner edge of the disc. This is why a CLV drive will suddenly speed up and get rather noisy.

A more important performance factor is the type of Constant Velocity technology used by the drive. Budget and mid-level models use Constant Linear Velocity (CLV), whereas top-end models use Constant Angular Velocity (CAV), or even a combination of the two. Check this out in the specifications.

Also, look for the drive's Access Time. This is measured in milli-seconds, and refers to the time needed to access a specific piece of data on the disc. The lower this is, the better.

The drive's buffer size is also important, as it is with hard drives. Top-end CD-ROM drives will have a buffer of 2 MB while cheaper models can have much less.

CD Writers

These devices are also known as "burners", as the writing process involves literally burning the data to the disc.

They come in two types – CD-R and CD-RW.

A CD-R (writer) drive will record to a "write-once-only" disc, known as a CD-R disc. Once these discs have been used, they cannot be used again.

There is little point in looking for a CD writer as opposed to a CD re-writer; perhaps in the hope of saving money (presuming if it does less, it will cost less). The fact is, these devices are now virtually obsolete, and nearly all writers currently on the market are re-writers.

CD-RW (re-writer) drives will record to CD-R discs and to CD-RW (re-writeable) discs.

CD-R discs are the most commonly used, and there are several reasons for this – they are the cheapest, the quickest to record to, and have a longer shelf life than CD-RWs. Due to differences in their composition, they are also more reliable than CD-RWs for data backup.

CD-R discs can be recorded to only once. However, they are cheap, quick and reliable.

CD-RW discs, on the other hand, can be reused a number of times. They do cost more though. In addition, recording to them can take three times longer than on CD-R discs.

For long-term data storage, always use CD-R discs.

The only real advantage CD-RWs hold over CD-Rs is the fact they can be reused – about a thousand times according to the manufacturers (as with all manufacturer claims, though, this needs to be taken with a pinch of salt).

In practice, there are only a few CD-R drives around now – virtually all of these devices are re-writables.

CD writers are packaged with various read and write speeds emblazoned across the box. Using the box below as an example, the first figure, 40X, is the speed at which the drive writes to a CD-R. 12X is the speed it writes to a CD-RW, and 48X is the

With regard CD drive speeds, the "X" stands for the transfer of 150 KB/s. So in the example opposite, the read speed of the drive is 7.8 MB (150 x 52).

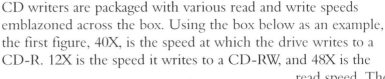

read speed. The higher these speeds, the better the drive's performance. The current speed standard is 52X, 32X, 52X.

When buying, you need to make sure the drive uses "burn proof"

technology. This is a feature designed to overcome a common failing in early CD writers called "buffer underrun". This happens when the flow of data to the drive during the write process is interrupted. The result is a failed "write" and a ruined disc. Burn proof technology prevents buffer underun and will be found on all good CD writers.

The aim of the Mount Rainier Initiative is to enable PC manufacturers to replace floppy disk and CD-ROM drives with one multi-function drive. This will read older CD-ROM, CD-R and CD-RW discs, write to CD-RW discs in the new Mount Rainier format, and also allow traditional mastering methods to be used.

Mount Rainier drives will allow the user to use the disc in exactly the same way they would a hard drive, i.e. drag-and-drop, saving to disc from an application's "Save" or "Save as" option, etc.

Several manufacturers have their own versions of burn proof technology, e.g. Seamless Link (Phillips), Safe Burn (Acer), JustLink (Ricoh) and Power Burn (Sony). Essentially, though, they all work in the same way and do the same thing.

A good-sized memory cache is also important and should be no less than 2 MB. Many top-end drives will have more.

Another thing to look for in your new drive is compliance with the Mount Rainier Initiative. This is a technology that allows users to record to a disc in exactly the same way they would with a hard or floppy drive, i.e. drag-and-drop, and no need for third-party mastering programs such as Nero. The purpose is to make CD writing much easier than it is at present.

DVD Drives

DVD (Digital Versatile Disc) drives are very similar in concept to CD-ROM drives. The basic difference is that DVD drives use a narrower laser for reading and writing that allows more tracks to be squeezed onto the discs. This vastly increases their storage capacity. In addition, the composition of a DVD disc allows two layers of data on each side, giving a theoretical maximum of some 18 GB. In practice though, most DVD discs currently on sale have a capacity of 4.7 GB, with 8.5 GB versions becoming increasingly common.

DVD Formats

While DVD drives are similar to CD drives in that both have read only (ROM), write (R) and re-write (RW) versions, the DVD market is enormously complicated by the fact that there are several different formats available. These are:

- DVD-ROM
- DVD-RAM
- DVD+R
- DVD-R
- DVD-RW
- DVD+RW

Each of these formats use a different type of disc, not all of which are compatible with the others, e.g. a DVD+R or DVD+RW drive can't write to a DVD-R or DVD-RW disc, and vice versa.

When making your choice of DVD drive, you need to first establish what you are going to use DVD for, e.g. burning music or video, watching commercially produced movies, data backup, etc. This will tell you which format to go for. Then you choose a drive that supports the chosen format.

The table below will point you in the right direction.

If your reason for buying a DVD drive is long-term data storage or system backup, DVD-RAM will be your best option. These discs are commonly housed in a protective caddy, much like a floppy or Zip disk. The drive itself also provides data protection techniques such as the marking of bad sectors. These features, plus a life expectancy of some 30 years, make DVD-RAM discs the most reliable of all the various formats.

Disc	Uses	Pros	Cons
DVD-ROM	Commercial movies, games, software	Plays on virtually all drives	Cannot be recorded to
DVD-RAM	Data backup	Offers drag-and-drop and fast data access. Most reliable of all the formats	Poor compatibility. Cannot be played on home-DVD players. Discs expensive
DVD-R and DVD-RW	Good for video discs. Also, audio discs, general data backup and transferral	High level of compatibility with other formats and home-DVD players	Lower maximum capacity than DVD+ discs. Write/read speeds are slower than DVD+
DVD+R and DVD+RW	Good for mixed data discs. Can also be used for video and audio discs	More video recording and editing features. Good level of compatibility with home-DVD players	Compatibility with other formats and home-DVD players lower than DVD-R/RW

If you cannot decide which DVD format to go for, just buy one of the multi-function drives. You will pay more though.

If all you want to do is watch commercial DVDs on your PC, a DVD-ROM drive will be the choice.

If you want DVD recording facilities, the choice is: DVD+, DVD- or DVD-RAM. DVD+ is the more advanced technology of the three, offers more in the way of data correction, and gives the user basic video-editing functions. It also offers faster read/write speeds.

DVD-RAM discs operate in a similar fashion to a hard disk and can be used in the same way. However, they can only be used in a DVD-RAM drive and are not compatible with the other formats. This severely limits your options.

Installing a Floppy Drive

The floppy drive fits at the top of the 3.5 inch drive bay assembly. Install it as follows:

Most system cases have only one floppy drive bay. However, this is identical to the hard drive bays, so before you start installing the drive, make sure you are using the right bay. Otherwise, you may find yourself doing it all again.

1 Slide the drive along the supporting shelves until the front is lined up with the front aperture of the case. Then screw it into place.

The floppy drive's power is supplied by the small 4-pin connector shown below. This is the smallest of the PSU's power connectors.

2 Connect the power connector to the socket at the left of the IDE socket.

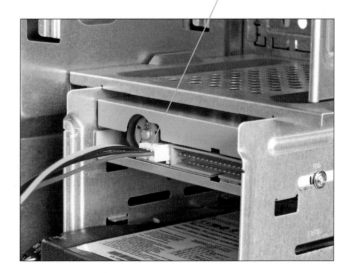

Floppy drive IDE cables have a twist in the middle at one end. This is the end that connects to the drive. The twist is there to ensure that you put the connectors in the correct sockets. The red stripe ensures you get the connectors the right way up – at the mainboard end, the stripe will be on the left, and at the drive end, it will be on the right.

When connecting the floppy drive you need to look at the cable. This will have a red stripe on one side, and also a twist in the middle at one end. The connector next to the twist goes to the drive, with the red stripe on the right-hand side. The other end goes to the mainboard with the stripe on the left-hand side. This is demonstrated below:

3 The drive connection with the twist next to the connector.

Unlike some floppy drives, hard drive and CD/DVD drive unit cable connectors are keyed. This makes it impossible to connect them incorrectly.

4 The mainboard connection with the red stripe on the left.

Installing a CD/DVD Drive

A CD/DVD drive is installed in one of the 5-inch drive bays at the top-front of the system case. Because this device is considerably larger than a hard or floppy drive, you may find it difficult, or even impossible, to install it from the inside as it may well be obstructed by the CPU heat sink/fan assembly, and maybe the PSU as well. In this case, removing the case's front cover will allow you to gain access to the drive bays from the front. The cover will be either clipped to the chassis or screwed to it from the inside. You may also be able to gain access by removing the top panel of the case, but you may as well do it from the front as you will need to remove the blanking plate before you can fit the drive.

Never try to force a CD/DVD drive into its bay if the path is obstructed. Instead, remove the appropriate blanking plate from the front panel (which you will have to do anyway), and then slide it in from there.

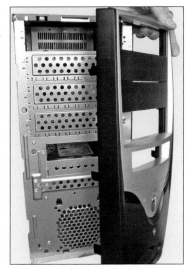

With the blanking plate removed, you will then be able to slide the drive unit into the case. When in place, secure it with the supplied screws and then replace the front cover.

You now need to connect the drive to the secondary IDE channel on the mainboard with an IDE cable. The socket for this channel is black, and it is situated next to the blue primary channel socket. Plug the blue end of the cable into the mainboard and the black end into the drive.

If you are installing two CD/DVD drives, perhaps one of each, they will have to be set up in a master/slave relationship. At the rear of the drive, you will find a jumper block that will allow you to do this.

Some CD/DVD drives support a technology known as Digital Audio Extraction (DAE). These drives do not need an audio cable connection to the sound system as the connection is made via the IDE/ATA bus. Read the documentation supplied with your drive to establish if this is the case with yours. If it is, you can dispense with the audio cable.

If you are using a sound card and want to play audio with your drive, it needs to be hooked up to the card. There will be a 4-pin analog cable supplied with the drive for this purpose. Connect one end to the drive, as shown below, and the other end to the appropriate socket on the sound card (you may need to consult the card's documentation to see where this is).

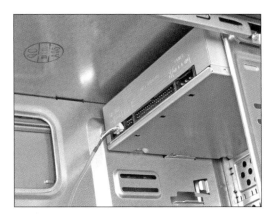

Peripherals

Peripheral devices extend the capabilities of a basic computer system and thus enable the user to do far more with it.

This chapter takes a look at the more common types, such as scanners, printers, etc. and explains what you need to look for to ensure you get a good quality device that will be suitable for your requirements.

NOTE: the installation procedures in this chapter cover the hardware installation. When the operating system is installed, the device drivers will also need to be installed.

Covers

Chapter Thirteen

Printers

When choosing your printer, pay attention to how it will connect to the PC. While virtually all printers these days have USB capability, so do most other types of peripheral. You may find you do not have enough USB ports available for all the devices you want to hook up. Therefore, it might be worth considering buying a printer with a parallel port connection to leave a USB port free for something else.

Ink-jets have never been so cheap to run as they are now. This is due to the rash of cartridge refill kits that, typically, offer some five times the amount of ink that you get with a new cartridge. There are also specialist stores where you can take the cartridges to be refilled.

You might also consider buying a dedicated photo printer. While considerably more expensive than a standard ink-jet, they do produce very high-quality prints.

As a cheaper alternative, there are ink-jet printers on the market for which it is possible to purchase a special photo-printing cartridge.

Ink-Jet Printers

Ink-jet printers are the type most commonly found in PC systems, and even low-end models are capable of producing high-quality

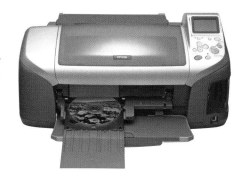

results. These devices are cheap to buy, but deliver high levels of performance.

The drawback with ink-jets is the high cost of the ink cartridges, although this has been negated to a large degree by the proliferation of ink-jet refill kits now on the market. If your printing needs are modest, an ink-jet is the one to go for. When buying an ink-jet printer, things to consider include:

Print Resolution – as even the cheapest printers can print at 1200 dpi, which is ample for most purposes, this will not be an issue for most people. However, high-resolution images will require a greater print resolution.

Print Speeds – usually quoted as pages per minute (PPM), for both color, and black & white. Obviously, the higher, the better.

Paper Handling – if you need to print on anything larger than the usual letter size or A4, will the printer accommodate it? Will it print on envelopes? Will the paper tray hold enough sheets for a long print job?

Physical Dimensions – if you have restricted desktop space it will be worth looking for a printer with a smaller "footprint".

Noise Level – these devices can be quite noisy, some much more than others. If you like as much peace and quiet as possible, look at the decibel rating.

Build Quality – one of the major differences between low- and top-end models is the build quality. If you buy from the lower end of the market, do not expect the printer to last forever.

Laser Printers

Laser technology is completely different from ink-jet and produces much better results in terms of print speed and quality. Laser

Until fairly recently, laser printers were just not viable for a home-PC environment due to their high cost. As with LCD monitors, though, the price of these devices has come down quite considerably, and they are now a serious alternative to the ubiquitous ink-jet.

While it might be difficult to justify the high cost of a color laser, a monochrome model will be a definite boon in a busy home office, or to those fed up with messing around with ink cartridges and head cleaning.

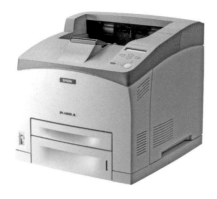

printers also offer more in the way of features, such as high-capacity paper trays and duplexing (the ability to print on both sides of the paper). They are also considerably cheaper to run.

The drawback is the high initial cost, although it must be said that low-end monochrome (black and white) lasers are now quite reasonably priced. They are also much more bulky than ink-jets.

However, if you envisage doing a large amount of printing, then a laser printer will very soon repay the initial cost.

If you decide to try one of these devices, apart from the considerations already mentioned on the previous page, you should also look at the following:

Toner and Drum – these are the two main consumables in a laser printer. With some lasers, the toner and drum are combined in a replaceable cartridge, while with others, they are separate parts. The problem with the cartridge type is that the toner will run out long before the drum needs replacing. However, some cartridges can be refilled with toner. To keep running costs down, avoid lasers which use a cartridge that cannot be refilled.

If you go for a laser printer, avoid the type that comes with a cartridge that cannot be refilled. While they will be cheaper, higher running costs will eventually cancel out any initial saving.

Memory – lasers, particularly low-end models, are often supplied with a minimal amount of memory, usually just enough to allow low-resolution printing. However, unlike ink-jets, many lasers include spare slots for memory upgrades – not all do, though, so if you intend printing graphics, check this out.

Also, find out if you can upgrade with cheaper generic memory, rather than having to use the manufacturer's brand which will be more expensive.

Installing a Printer

Your printer connects to the PC via either the Parallel Port or a USB port, depending on which type of printer you have. In the example below, we are using the author's trusty Epson, which is a Parallel Port ink-jet.

When installing a Parallel Port printer, it's quite common for a scanner or Zip drive to be also connected to the Parallel port. This is possible because Parallel Port devices have two sockets – data in and data out. For this to work, however, the cables must be connected to the correct sockets. For example, if you are connecting a printer and a Zip drive, connect the printer to the input socket of the Zip drive, and connect the Zip drive's output to the PC's Parallel Port socket.

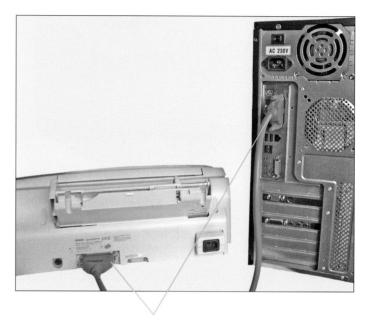

One end of the cable goes to the printer and the other end to the PC's Parallel Port socket (see page 55).

Modems

A modem with voice facilities is capable of playing and recording audio over a telephone line. With a suitable software package, such a modem can be configured to act as a telephone answering machine. While not earth-shattering in concept, it is cheaper than buying a dedicated answering machine.

You should also ensure your modem has a FLASH memory chip, as opposed to a ROM chip. A FLASH chip will enable you to update the modem periodically, by downloading a firmware upgrade from the manufacturer's website. NOTE: FLASH upgrades can be obtained for many other peripheral devices as well, such as scanners, printers and digital cameras.

To be able to use the Modem-on-hold facility of a V.92 modem, the feature also needs to be supported by the ISP.

If you want to access the Internet with your new PC, you will need to buy a modem. These come in two types – Dial-up and Broadband.

Dial-up Modems

These devices are rated in standards, such as V.34, V.42, V.44, V.90 and V.92.

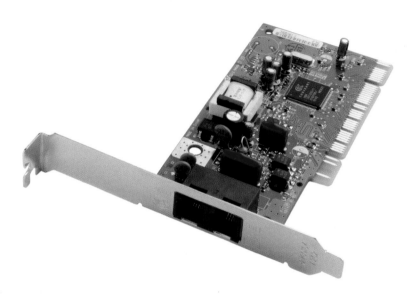

The V.90 standard was the first to offer data transfer rates of 56 KB, and this is still the fastest rate currently available. V.90 has now been superseded by V.92. While this works at 56 KB as well, it adds several new features, the main ones being "Quick Connect" and "Modem-on-Hold". As a result, V.92 represents a significant improvement over V.90.

- Quick Connect halves the time needed to establish a connection.

- Modem-on-Hold allows you to receive an incoming call without breaking the connection to the Internet. Furthermore, you can make a telephone call while connected to the Internet without losing the connection.

Something else you might consider is buying a modem which offers fax and voice facilities.

Broadband Modems

If broadband is available in your area, then you ought to seriously consider signing up for it. It has many advantages and will revolutionize the way you use the Internet.

- Your connection will always be on.

- File download and site connection speeds will be many times faster (depending on which package you sign-up for).

- You won't suffer from periodic breaks in the connection as you do with a dial-up connection.

- Your telephone line won't be tied up.

Broadband comes in several versions, each of which require the use of a specialized modem.

- ISDN – works on telephone lines with speeds up to 128 KB/s.

- DSL and ADSL – works on telephone lines with speeds up to 10 MB/s, although few ISPs offer anything higher than 1.5 MB/s.

- Cable – works on CATV cable networks and provides similar speeds to DSL and ADSL.

Virtually all ISPs will supply a modem as part of the package (and charge you rental accordingly), so this is not something you need to consider, unless of course, you buy your own modem, which may allow you to negotiate a lower price with the ISP.

Of the three types, cable is the recommended option as it is the easiest to set up. However, not everyone has access to a cable network, and if this is the case, DSL is the next best option.

If you go for a cable modem, you will find the connection to the computer will be either USB or Ethernet. For simplicity of installation, USB is by far the easiest. An Ethernet connection will also require an Ethernet PCI card to be installed and set up in the PC.

Installing a Modem

Dial-up Modems

The procedure is the same as for any PCI card.

Dial-up modems are also available as external models. Apart from being easier to install, they also allow the user to see what the modem is doing by observing the front panel lights. They do cost more though.

1 Slip the card into the slot and screw the face plate to the chassis.

2 Then take the supplied cable and plug one end into the telephone socket and the other into the modem's Phone socket.

Cable Modems

Virtually all cable modems are now supplied with the USB interface. Installation is a breeze; just plug in the USB cable. If you are using an Ethernet connection, you will have to also install an Ethernet PCI card in the PC.

Your cable modem will require a short period in which to "settle" down before it can be used. This is indicated by the front panel lights flashing randomly.

Note that cable modems have to go through an initialization routine before they are ready to go. With some of these devices, this procedure can take anything up to 20 minutes, although newer cable modems do it much more quickly. In any event, you will know that the modem is ready when the LEDs on the front panel stop flashing.

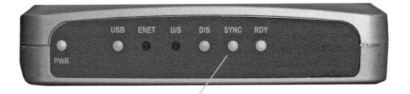

Front panel lights flash until modem is ready

Scanners

Scanning, particularly at high-resolutions, is not the quickest thing you will ever do on your PC. If this is something you do a lot of, be wary of USB powered scanners.

These devices draw their power from the USB BUS, which is not too generous in this respect, so by necessity, the scanner motor is a low-powered affair. That translates into slow scans.

Make sure any USB scanner you buy is AC powered.

Scanners are devices that are by no means essential, but can turn out to be surprisingly useful in many ways. For home-users, the flatbed type (shown below) is the best one to go for.

When deciding which scanner to buy, you need to consider the following specifications:

Never buy a scanner on the basis of manufacturers' advertising claims of scan resolutions as high as 12,800 dpi. Scanners are simply not capable of picking up this level of detail.

What the manufacturers are referring to is image "Interpolation", which is a process that the scanning software uses to supposedly increase the resolution of an image. It does this by creating extra pixels in-between the ones actually scanned. In short, it is basically guesswork and serves no practical purpose.

If your scanner is capable of 600 dpi, that's probably all you will ever need.

Color Depth – this defines how many colors a scanner can register and is measured in bits. 36-bits is the minimum you want to accept and will produce good results for most applications.

Optical Resolution – this is the maximum number of dots per inch (dpi) that the scanner can register, and the higher this figure, the better the reproduction of the scanned image or document. 600 dpi will be fine for most purposes. However, documents to be professionally printed may need a resolution of at least 2400 dpi. NOTE: completely ignore figures quoted for "Enhanced" or "Interpolated resolution" – see margin note opposite.

Interface – SCSI (requires a SCSI adapter) is the ideal for speed. Next best is USB (USB2 ideally). Avoid Parallel Port, as this is the slowest interface, and furthermore, can interfere with the printer.

Scanning Area – if you need to scan large documents, buy a scanner with a larger scanning bed.

Accessories – some scanners can be bought with accessories such as slide and negative attachments, and sheet feeders.

Speakers

The wider a speaker's frequency range is, the better its quality. Low-frequency response is essential for good bass reproduction, while high-frequency response is essential for good treble reproduction.

Connect a $2000 sound card to a $20 speaker system and you will get $20 worth of sound quality. If you want high-fidelity, or in the case of the gamer, good 3D Surround Sound, then you must buy an appropriate set of speakers together with a suitable sound system. High quality reproduction is determined by the following speaker specifications:

Frequency response – this is measured in Hertz and a typical range will be about 33 Hz to 20 KHz. For this to have any meaning, remember that humans can hear from 20 Hz up to 20 KHz. The closer to these thresholds the speaker's frequency response range is, the better the bass and treble reproduction.

Sensitivity – often referred to as Sound Pressure Level or SPL in specification sheets. Measured in decibels, a typical figure is about 90 DB. The higher this figure, the better.

Those who need plenty of volume will be interested in the speaker's wattage rating. This tells you how much power the speakers can take without damage. The higher this figure, the louder you can play them.

If the thought of having Surround Sound appeals to you, remember that the speaker system will need to be supported by the computer. Some current integrated sound systems can support 5.1 sound; any higher than this though will require a dedicated sound card.

Games and DVD movies will benefit enormously from Surround Sound speaker systems. However, these need to be supported by the PC's sound system.

Don't forget to check that the cabling supplied with the speaker system will cover all your requirements. For example, digital optical cables for DVD and CD drives are often sold separately.

Speaker Installation

Many sound cards provide color-coded input and output jacks for easy identification. These are:

Green – Line out
Orange – Line out
Black – Line out
Blue – Line in
Pink – Microphone

In multiple-speaker setups, the green line out jack is used for the front speakers, the black jack for the rear speakers, and the orange jacks for the center and side speakers.
  Note that not all sound cards are color coded in this way – it is not a standard.

This is a simple enough exercise. However, it is remarkable how many people get it wrong, connecting the speakers to either the wrong sound system (integrated instead of the sound card or vice versa), or to the wrong socket. The input/output ports of a standard sound card are shown below.

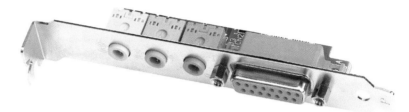

From left to right, these are: Line Out, Line In, Mic (microphone input) and Midi port

The speakers connect to the green line out jack. Use any other jack and you will not get any sound from the PC. With this type of card, you will only be able to use a two-speaker setup.

Advanced sound cards offer more in the way of connectivity as demonstrated by the input/output panel of the card shown below:

S/PDIF stands for Sony/Philips Digital Interface; a standard audio file transfer format. Developed jointly by the Sony and Phillips corporations, S/PDIF allows the transfer of digital audio signals from one device to another without having to be first converted to an analog format, which has a degrading effect on the quality of the signal.

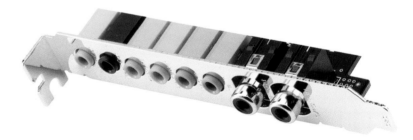

Here, the green, black and two orange jacks all provide a line out connection. The pink jack is for a microphone, the blue jack is for line in, and finally, there are input and output sockets for S/PDIF coaxial cables.

This type of card is suitable for running multiple-speaker setups; the card shown above can support eight speakers.

Zip Drives

ZIP disks come in the following versions:

- 100 MB capacity
- 250 MB capacity
- 750 MB capacity

Internal and external drive models are available, although the usual caveat applies to the external models – higher prices.

Also available from Iomega is the Rev Drive, disks for which can hold up to 35 GB of data. However, its cost is considerable – you

could buy a 60 GB IDE internal hard drive for the same amount. The advantage of the Rev disk, of course, is the fact that it's portable.

ZIP/Rev disks also have the advantage of being very robust, and thus, are a reliable storage medium. They are also much simpler to use than writeable CDs as you can drag-and-drop in the same way you would with a hard drive.

Another plus for Zip drives is that the software supplied with them allows the user to password-protect the disks – a feature that can be useful.

Game Controllers

Before buying a controller, consider the types of game you are likely to be playing.

Joysticks will get the best out of flight simulators and will be adequate for racing games.

However, if you play a lot of racing games, and can put up with the pitying looks you will inevitably receive, a dedicated steering wheel and foot pedal setup is what you need.

Gamepads are the best choice for all-round use.

Those of you who are into computer games definitely need to check out the wide range of high-quality controllers that are available. The cheap and nasty affairs that are commonly supplied with pre-built systems will not cut the mustard with today's games.

For strategy games such as Age of Empires and Sim City, all you need is your keyboard. However, while this will be adequate, a better option is to invest in a specialized gaming keyboard. You will find more details regarding these devices on page 121.

These devices come in three main types: joysticks, steering-wheels and gamepads. Which type you buy depends on the games you want to play. Each of them has characteristics and features that suit specific types of game.

Joysticks (a nice example is shown above), are ideally suited to action games like flight simulators and racing games.

Steering-wheels, as you might imagine, are intended for use with racing games like Formula One and NASCAR.

Serious action gaming will subject controllers to a lot of punishment – make sure that the one you buy will be up to it. While they all look great in the advertising photos, in the flesh, they are sometimes not quite so impressive.

A good bit of advice is to buy your controller from a store where you can have a good look at it. By picking up these devices and clicking the buttons, you'll soon sort the good from the bad.

Gamepads are all-rounders, and incorporate controls that allow you to adequately play any type of action game.

When evaluating these devices, look for the following features:

Build quality – game controllers take a lot of hammer, so they need to be sturdily constructed.

Force feedback – this simulates G-forces, bumps, etc, and lets you "feel it" when you crash your racing car at 160 mph.

Twist handle (joysticks) – this provides a realistic rudder control in a flight game.

Number of buttons – the more of these you have, the greater the control you have over the game.

Setting Up the System

This is the final stage of building your computer, and for the uninitiated, probably the trickiest.

To get the computer operational, there are quite a few changes that need to be made to the default BIOS settings. This chapter shows you exactly what you must do in this respect.

Then, the hard drive has to be partitioned and formatted.

Finally, you need to install the operating system. Windows XP is currently the most popular of these, and so is what we will use to demonstrate the procedure.

Covers

Chapter Fourteen

The BIOS

The BIOS (basic input-output system) is a chip located on the mainboard, which handles all the startup routines necessary to get the computer running. These include checking that crucial parts, such as the memory, video system and hard drive are working correctly, checking to see what other hardware is in the system, and finally, loading the operating system.

Setting up your new system comprises three stages:

1) Configuring the following components in the BIOS:

- Floppy drive
- Hard drive
- Boot device
- USB
- Disabling integrated sound (if necessary)
- AGP video card (if installed)
- The Date and Time

2) Partitioning and formatting the hard drive.

3) Installing the operating system.

The BIOS setup program is accessed by switching on the computer, and as the first boot screen loads, holding down a key. This is usually the Delete key but some BIOS programs may require a different key. This is specified at the bottom of the boot screen as shown below.

Some BIOS programs use a different key to enter Setup. These are usually the F1, F2 or Esc keys. In all cases though, the required key will be specified on the boot screen.

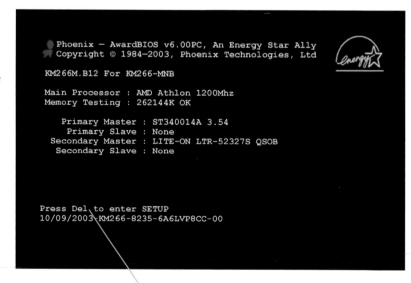

BIOS Setup program entry key

Before you can start making changes in the BIOS, you need to be able to navigate your way around. The table below shows you how:

To navigate your way around the various BIOS menus, use the Esc and Arrow keys. To change settings, use the Page Up and Page Down keys.

Up arrow key	moves the cursor up
Down arrow key	moves the cursor down
Left arrow key	moves the cursor left
Right arrow key	moves the cursor right
Page Up key	selects a higher value
Page Down key	selects a lower value
Enter key	makes a selection
Escape key	returns to the previous menu
F1	Opens the BIOS Help screen

Setting Up the Floppy Drive

Enter the BIOS Setup program as described on page 158.

Before closing the BIOS Setup program, you must save any changes you have made. If you don't, they will revert to the original settings.

Using the arrow keys on the keyboard, scroll to Standard CMOS Features and hit Enter.

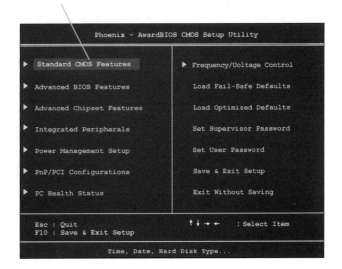

2 Scroll down to "None", opposite Drive A.

Some BIOS programs automatically detect and configure the floppy drive. However, many do not, in which case you should follow the procedure detailed on this page.

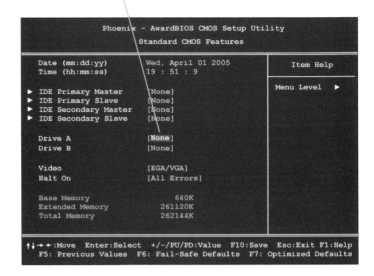

3 Then, use the Page Up/Page Down keys to select the "1.44M 3.5 in" option. This is the floppy drive.

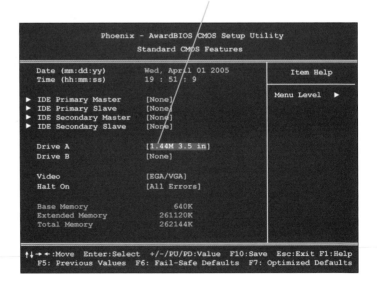

4 Hit the Esc key to return to the main BIOS page.

Setting the Boot Device

A boot device is a device that must be initialized prior to loading the operating system. This includes the primary input device (keyboard), the primary output device (display) and the initial program load device (hard, floppy or CD drive).

Having initialized the system's hardware, the BIOS then searches the system's drives for the operating system. The order in which it does this must be specified by the user. Do it as follows:

The order in which your system searches your drives for the operating system is set in the BIOS. The usual configuration is:

1) Floppy drive
2) Hard drive
3) CD-ROM drive

However, there may be situations that require a different configuration. The installation of Windows XP is an example. This requires the CD-ROM drive to be set as the boot device.

1   On the main BIOS page, select Advanced BIOS Features and hit Enter.

2   On the next page, scroll down to First Boot Device. Using the Page Up/Page Down keys, select "Floppy".

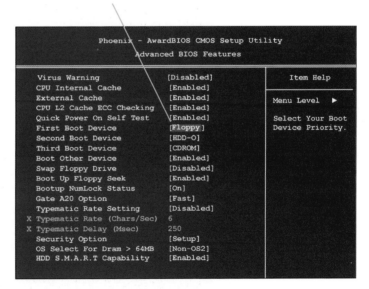

3   Then, select Second Boot Device and set this to "HDD-0".

4   Finally, select Third Boot Device and set this to "CDROM".

5   Hit the Escape key to return to the main BIOS page.

Setting Up the Hard Drive

Open the Standard CMOS Features page and do the following:

As with floppy drives, some BIOS programs will automatically detect and configure a hard drive when it is installed in a system. If this is the case, you will see the drive listed on the first boot screen, next to the IDE channel used.

1 Scroll down to IDE Primary Master and hit Enter.

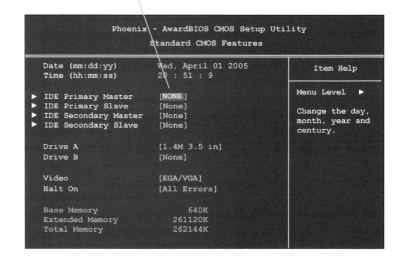

2 This will open the hard drive Auto-Detection page. Scroll to IDE HDD Auto-Detection and press Enter.

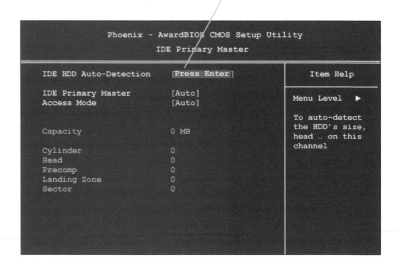

The BIOS will now detect the hard drive's parameters and display them as shown below:

Under the IDE Auto-Detection setting, there is another one called IDE Primary Master. This is set to "Auto" by default. What this means is that every time the computer is booted, the BIOS will automatically re-detect the hard drive. By highlighting the setting and pressing Enter, you will see a Manual option. This allows you to enter the drive's parameters manually (you'll find these in the documentation or printed on the drive's casing). If the BIOS doesn't detect these parameters with the Auto-Detect option, try entering them manually.

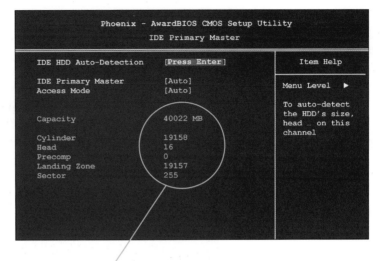

3 Hard drive's parameters. Hit the Escape key and you will be returned to the Standard CMOS Features page.

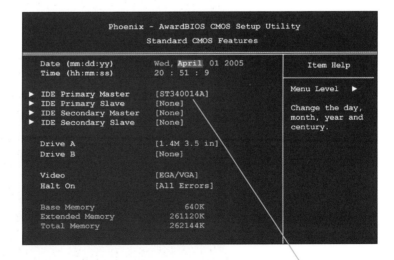

4 Your hard drive will now be listed in the IDE Primary Master category. This indicates it has been successfully set up.

Enabling USB

If you intend running any USB devices, you will need to enable USB in the BIOS.

After enabling USB in your BIOS, you will also need to install a USB driver for any USB devices you want to run. If you are using Windows XP, you may need to download an XP-compatible USB driver from the manufacturer's website.

On the main BIOS page, select Integrated Peripherals and press Enter.

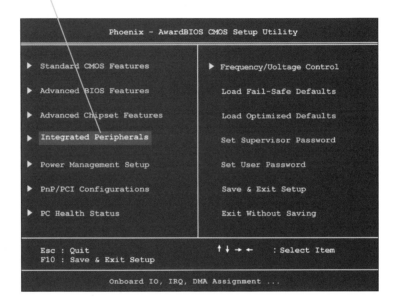

Scroll to "Via Onchip PCI Device" and press Enter.

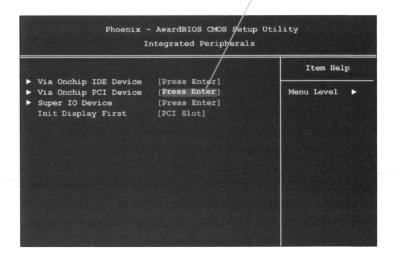

3 Scroll to OnChip USB Controller and select "Enabled".

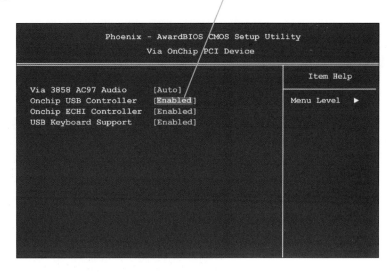

If you intend using a sound card in your computer, you must disable the mainboard's integrated sound system. This is enabled by default.

Disabling Integrated Sound

If you have decided to install a sound card, then you must disable the integrated sound system. Do it as follows:

With the "Via OnChip PCI Device" menu still open, scroll up to VIA-3858 AC97 Audio and select "Disabled".

In the example opposite, the integrated sound system is the 3858 AC97 Audio, which is incorporated in the Via chipset on the mainboard.

Unless, by some chance, your mainboard uses the same chipset, the BIOS in your system will read slightly differently.

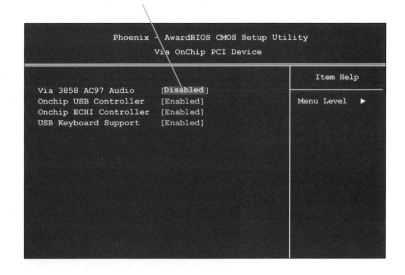

Setting Up an AGP Video Card

If you are installing a video card, you do not need to disable the integrated video (if any) – this is done automatically. If it is an AGP card, however, then you do need to set it up in the BIOS.

The situation regarding the disabling of mainboard integrated systems is different with video than it is with sound. Whereas a sound card will not work until any integrated sound system has been disabled, the installation of a video card will automatically disable an integrated video system.

If a video card is removed from a computer then integrated video (if present) will be automatically re-enabled.

On the main BIOS page, select Advanced Chipset Features and hit Enter.

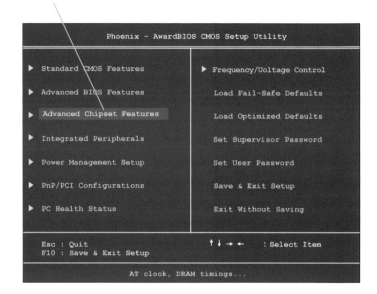

Scroll down to AGP & P2P Bridge Control and hit Enter.

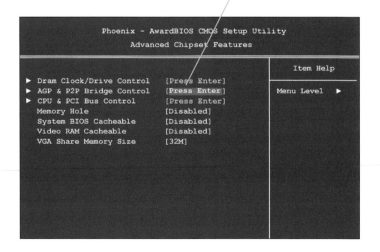

3 Scroll to AGP Aperture Size and set it to half your installed RAM. For example, if you have 512 MB of RAM, select 256M.

An AGP Aperture Size of half the installed RAM is the generally accepted setting. However, this isn't written in stone and a different setting might be better for your setup. You can experiment with this, but initially, set it to half.

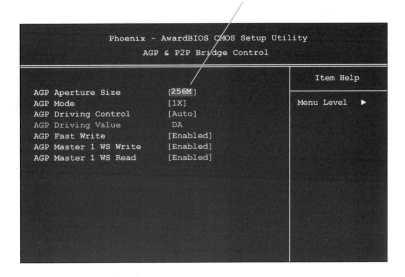

4 Finally, scroll to AGP Mode and select the AGP acceleration factor of your card, i.e. 1X, 2X, 4X or 8X.

Your video card's acceleration factor will be emblazoned across the box. Alternatively, it will be in the enclosed documentation.

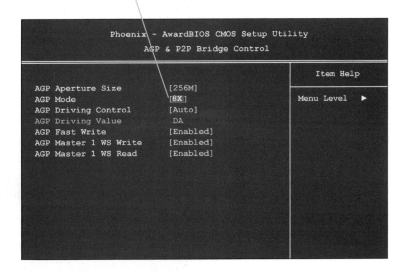

Setting the Date and Time

This may have already been done by the manufacturer. If not, do it as described below.

1 On the main BIOS page, select Standard CMOS Features.

The mainboard's manufacturer may have set the date and time already. This is possible as there is a battery on the mainboard, which maintains power to the BIOS chip at all times, even when the board is sitting on the retailer's shelf.

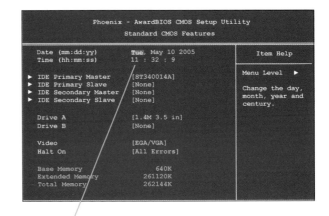

2 Scroll to Date and Time, respectively, and enter the correct figures using the Page Up/Page Down keys.

Now you need to save all the changes you have made in the BIOS.

1 Return to the main BIOS screen and scroll to Save and Exit Setup. Hit Enter and then Y to confirm.

When exiting the BIOS program, you must save your changes as shown opposite. Otherwise, they will revert to the original settings.

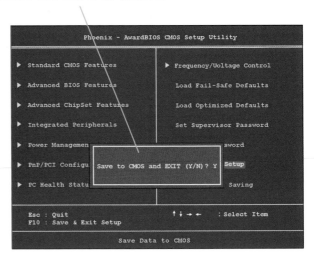

Partitioning and Formatting

Before any hard disk drive can be used, it has to be partitioned and formatted.

Neglecting to do this is a common mistake made by people when replacing, or adding a drive to their system.

If you don't do it, while the drive will be recognized by the system, it won't be by the operating system.

Before you can use your hard drive, it must be partitioned and then formatted. The way you go about doing this depends on which version of Windows you are installing.

If it is Windows 95, 98, Me, NT 4.0 or 2000, you will need a startup disk that contains the partitioning and formatting tools. This is a separate procedure carried out before installing Windows.

However, if you intend to run Windows XP, partitioning and formatting is part of the installation procedure (on a new system). As XP is all the rage at the moment, this is what we'll use here.

Before you can use XP's installation disk though, you must first set the CD-ROM drive as the first boot device. Do this as follows:

1 Start the PC and access the BIOS Setup program as described on page 158. Open the Advanced BIOS Features page and scroll down to First Boot Device.

Partitioning is the process of defining specific areas of the hard disk for the operating system to use.

Formatting prepares a disk to receive data by organizing it into logical units called blocks, sectors and tracks. These enable the drive's read/write heads to accurately locate data.

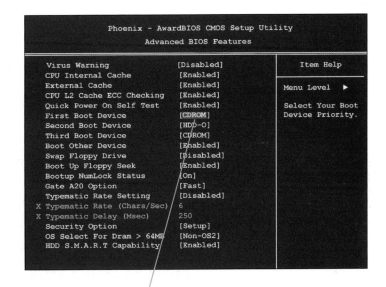

2 Using the Page Up/Page Down keys, select CDROM, save the change and exit the BIOS.

Installing Windows XP

Having set the CD-ROM drive as the first boot device, place the XP installation disk in the CD drive and boot the PC. At the bottom of the second boot screen, you will see a message saying "Press any key to boot from CD...". Do so, and after a short period, you'll see the following screen:

With Windows XP, the installation CD is the boot disk. This means that you have to set the CD-ROM drive as the first boot device. Earlier versions of Windows operating systems need a boot floppy disk for installation. This disk contains the partitioning and formatting tools, plus a generic CD-ROM driver.

XP provides everything you need on the installation disk.

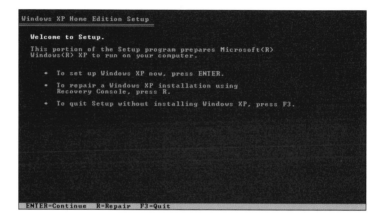

Hit Enter to begin the XP installation.

First though, you need to accept the license agreement by pressing the F8 key.

3 If you are using an upgrade version, then you'll need to prove that you have owned a full version of Windows at some point by placing it in the CD drive. Otherwise, you won't see this screen.

If you are installing Windows XP Home or Professional with an upgrade CD, be sure to have your qualifying media to hand. This can be a retail Windows 98, 98 SE, Millennium Edition (Me), NT 4.0 or 2000 CD-ROM.

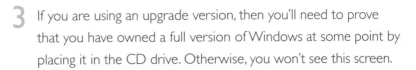

4 Next, you will see a screen showing available installation options, i.e. where XP can be installed. Because the hard drive is new and hasn't been partitioned yet, all you will see is unpartitioned space equal to the size of the drive.

If you are unfamiliar with partitioning procedures, accept XP's default partition setting, i.e. one partition equal to the full size of the disk.

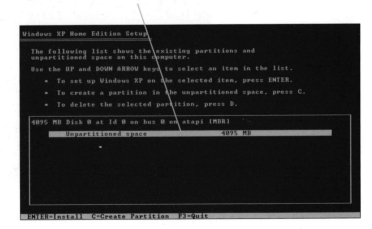

At this stage, you have two options. First, if you press Enter, XP will automatically create a single partition equal to the size of the drive. If you do this, you will then be taken directly to the format screen as shown on the next page.

...cont'd

XP allows you to format the drive in one of two file systems – NTFS or FAT. Unless you are planning to make use of XP's multi-boot facility that allows two or more operating systems to be installed on the PC, choose the NTFS option. Without going into the reasons, this will be the best choice.

You also have the option of doing a "Quick" format. Only use this if the drive is brand new, as this option does not check the disk for errors such as bad sectors.

5. Select the file system you want to use – FAT or NTFS – and press Enter. XP will then format the newly created partition.

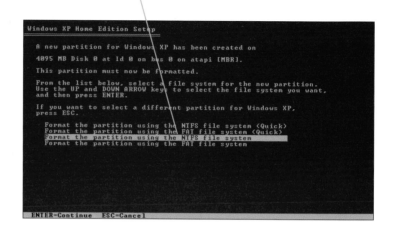

However, if you want to create two or more partitions, then press C in Step 4 on page 171. You will see the partitioning screen shown below.

The "Quick" format option will take a few seconds, literally. The "Full" format option, however, can take a long time. The larger the drive's capacity, the longer it will take.

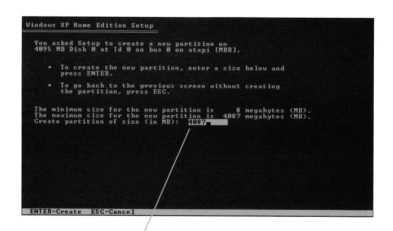

6. Here, there are options for creating one or more partitions in sizes of your own choice.

Once the disk has been partitioned and formatted, the installation routine will automatically begin copying files to the hard drive.

During this procedure, you will see various screens, such as Regional and Language settings, that allows you to choose your time zone and keyboard layout. At some stage, you will also be asked to enter the product key.

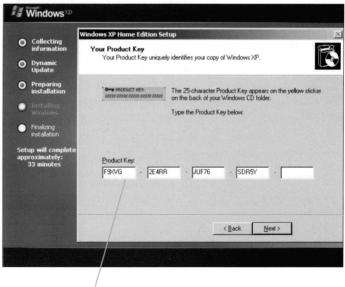

7 Type in the XP product key and click Next.

If you intend to do any networking, you need to give the computer a name when prompted to do so. At the final screen you will be given network settings options.

You can now sit back as the installation procedure completes. Finally, you will see the XP Desktop.

With a well-specified system, the installation of Windows XP should take about twenty minutes. However, if Setup grinds to a halt, it will be because there is a problem with the hardware you have installed. XP does have compatibility issues with certain hardware devices, video cards in particular.

In this situation, remove as much of the hardware as you can before retrying the installation. Devices you can remove are sound, network, modem and SCSI cards. Also, remove any USB devices with the exception of the mouse and keyboard. If the mainboard has an integrated video system, you can remove the video card as well (remember to relocate the VGA cable accordingly), otherwise, you'll have to leave it in. Then run Setup again.

With the system up and running, the next thing you need to do is install the drivers for your sound and video systems.

While XP will automatically install a video driver, this will be a generic driver that will not provide optimum performance. To get the best out of your video system, you must install the driver supplied with it.

At this stage, you also need to select the optimum refresh rate. By default, XP will choose a low refresh rate, often 60 Hz. This will cause the display to flicker. Change this by right-clicking the desktop, and selecting Properties, the Settings tab, Advanced and Monitor. Under Monitor Settings, select the highest refresh rate available.

Finally, install the drivers for all the peripheral devices you have installed.

Troubleshooting

If all goes to plan, you won't need to read this chapter. However, you'll have done well if everything works perfectly at the first time of asking.

It is more likely that you'll experience a problem or two somewhere along the way, and the purpose of this chapter is to provide a solution if you do.

Covers

Chapter Fifteen

Hard Drives

Hard Drive Failure

When you boot the computer, on the first boot screen you should see the hard drive listed next to "Primary Master" as shown below:

If the drive is recognized by the BIOS, this is a good indicator that the drive itself is ok. In this situation, a disk boot error message is a likely indication of a problem with the operating system. It may have to be reinstalled.

```
  Phoenix — AwardBIOS v6.00PC, An Energy Star Ally
  Copyright © 1984-2003, Phoenix Technologies, Ltd

  KM266M.B12 For KM266-MNB

  Main Processor : AMD Athlon 1200Mhz
  Memory Testing : 262144K OK

     Primary Master : ST340014A 3.54
      Primary Slave : None
   Secondary Master : LITE-ON LTR-52327S QSOB
    Secondary Slave : None


  Press Del to enter SETUP
  10/09/2003-KM266-8235-6A6LVP8CC-00
```

If you don't, the PC isn't "seeing" it. Depending on the mainboard in your system, one of two things will happen.

1) Boot-up will stop at this point.

2) Boot-up will continue and then stop with a "Disk Boot Failure" error message as shown below.

If the system doesn't recognize the hard drive, the most likely cause of the problem is a loose or incorrect connection. When rooting about in the case fitting other devices, it is quite possible that you have inadvertently loosened one of the drive's IDE connectors, or its power connector.

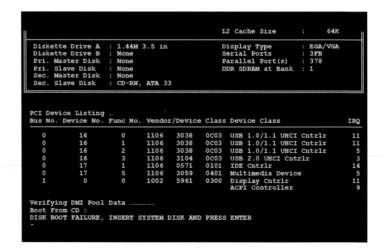

```
                                   L2 Cache Size      :    64K
  Diskette Drive A  : 1.44M 3.5 in    Display Type     : EGA/VGA
  Diskette Drive B  : None            Serial Ports     : 3FB
  Pri. Master Disk  : None            Parallel Port(s) : 378
  Pri. Slave Disk   : None            DDR SDRAM at Bank : 1
  Sec. Master Disk  : None
  Sec. Slave Disk   : CD-RW, ATA 33


  PCI Device Listing …
  Bus No. Device No. Func No. Vendor/Device Class Device Class         IRQ
       0       16        0     1106   3038   0C03  USB 1.0/1.1 UHCI Cntrlr  11
       0       16        1     1106   3038   0C03  USB 1.0/1.1 UHCI Cntrlr  11
       0       16        2     1106   3038   0C03  USB 1.0/1.1 UHCI Cntrlr   5
       0       16        3     1106   3104   0C03  USB 2.0 UHCI Cntrlr       3
       0       17        1     1106   0571   0101  IDE Cntrlr               14
       0       17        5     1106   3059   0401  Multimedia Device         5
       1        0        0     1002   5961   0300  Display Cntrlr           11
                                                   ACPI Controller           9

  Verifying DMI Pool Data ……………………
  Boot From CD :
  DISK BOOT FAILURE, INSERT SYSTEM DISK AND PRESS ENTER
  _
```

There are four possible reasons for this:

- The drive is not getting any power
- The drive has been incorrectly installed
- The drive is not configured in the BIOS
- The drive is faulty

The first thing to check is that the drive is getting power from the power supply unit. The easiest way to do this is to connect a different power connector that you know is working. You can use the one powering the CD drive.

Next, check that the drive is properly connected to the mainboard.

If there's still no joy, check its configuration in the BIOS (see pages 162-163). If the BIOS doesn't recognize the drive's parameters, then it is faulty and will need replacing.

Another problem that can occur is the boot procedure stopping at the "Verifying DMI Pool Data" stage, as shown below.

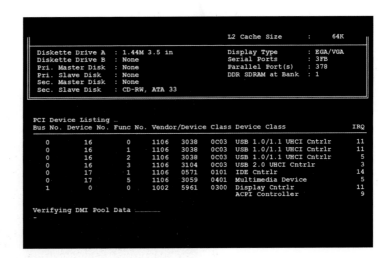

This may be the result of a transient configuration problem that can usually be repaired by switching off and then back on again.

If the problem persists, it is likely to be a connection issue. Open the system case and check that the IDE cable is securely connected to both the mainboard and hard drive.

Removable Media Drives

CD and DVD Drives

If the device is not listed on the first boot screen next to the IDE channel on which it was installed, then it hasn't been installed correctly. Open the case and check the IDE connections. Also check that the drive is getting power. If the system still doesn't recognize it, then it is faulty and will need replacing.

If you have installed two or more CD/DVD drives in the system, and one or both don't work, check that you have correctly positioned the master/slave configuration jumpers at the rear of the units.

If the computer is recognizing the drive but the operating system isn't, then you have a hardware conflict issue that is beyond the scope of this book. However, this usually means that the device is using the same IRQ (Interrupt ReQuest code) as another device. This type of problem can usually be resolved in the Device Manager. It could also be a driver issue but this is much less likely.

Floppy Drives

An issue peculiar to some floppy drives is that the IDE socket in some units is not keyed (the key is a little cut-out which accepts a matching lug on the connector to ensure the cable is connected the right way round). Because of this, it is possible to seemingly connect the floppy drive to the mainboard correctly when, in fact, the connector is the wrong way round.

If you get a "Floppy disk fail" error message, you probably have the IDE connector fitted upside down. Try it the other way and the problem should be resolved. Also, if the drive's LED is on permanently, this is a sure indicator of an incorrectly fitted cable.

If you see the following on boot-up, check this out.

Boot-up has stopped with a "Floppy disk fail" error message. Pressing the F1 key gives you the option to resume boot-up

Video

Blank Display

If the boot procedure gets as far as the point where Windows begins to load, and then the screen goes blank, the cause is likely to be an AGP video card incorrectly configured in the BIOS. If you find yourself in this situation, do the following:

Theoretically, the AGP Aperture Size should be set to half the amount of RAM installed in the system, i.e. "256M" for 512 MB of RAM, "128M" for 256 MB of RAM, etc.

In practice, though, this doesn't always work, and you may have to try different figures.

1 Reboot into the BIOS Setup program – see page 158.

2 Select Advanced Chipset Features and press Enter.

3 At the next screen, select AGP & P2P Bridge Control.

4 Highlight AGP Aperture Size.

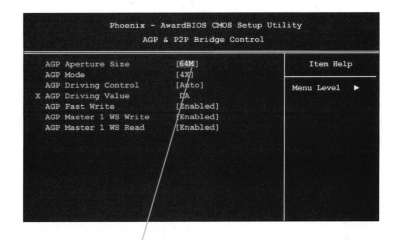

In case you are wondering, the AGP Aperture Size setting determines how much of the system's memory the video card will use once it's own memory has been used.

5 Use the Page Up/Page Down keys to select the [64M] option.

6 Save the changes and exit the BIOS.

7 Reboot, and the problem should now be resolved. Repeat steps 1 to 5 to find the highest AGP Aperture Size your system can handle, rebooting after each change.

Display is Scrambled

When Windows starts, instead of seeing the desktop, all you see is a scrambled display, i.e. a mass of unintelligible lines. This is indicative of an incorrectly configured video card. Resolve it as follows:

If you have a video problem that you cannot resolve, try the following:
Reboot, and enter the BIOS Setup program. At the opening page, scroll to "Load Fail-Safe Defaults". Press Enter, save the change, exit the BIOS and reboot. This procedure loads settings that should work with any system setup. NOTE: this will undo all the changes you have made in the BIOS during the setting-up procedure. If the video is now restored, you will have to redo them.

1   Reboot the PC and go to "Startup Options" by tapping the F8 key as the PC boots.

```
Windows Advanced Options Menu
Please select an option:

    Safe Mode
    Safe Mode with Networking
    Safe Mode with Command Prompt

    Enable Boot Logging
    Enable VGA Mode
    Last Known Good Configuration (your most recent settings that worked)
    Directory Services Restore Mode (Windows domain controllers only)
    Debugging Mode
    Disable Automatic Restart on System Failure

    Start Windows Normally
    Reboot
    Return to OS Choices Menu

Use the up and down arrow keys to move the highlight to your choice
```

2   Use the arrow keys to select "Enable VGA Mode" and hit Enter.

If you have installed Windows XP on your system, as soon as you have it up and running, go to Display Properties and set the refresh rate to the highest setting available.

The PC will continue to boot, and this time the display should be restored. If it is, when in Windows, install the driver that was supplied with the card, and then reboot the system again. This problem can occur with certain makes of video cards when used in conjunction with Windows XP.

If the above procedure doesn't work, then reboot the PC and go back to Startup Options as described above. This time select "Safe Mode" and hit Enter. When back in Windows, right-click the desktop, click Properties, Settings and Advanced. Then click the Monitor tab. Under Monitor Settings, you will see a drop-down box that allows you to change the refresh rate. Select the highest one available and then reboot the system. On restart, the display should be restored.

Sound

If the computer isn't communicating with you audibly, the first thing to check is that the sound system is correctly installed.

| In the Control Panel, click Sounds and Audio Devices.

Computer sound systems are well known for failing – the usual cause being a bad driver. These are very susceptible to crashes and incorrect shutdowns, etc. and are thus easily corrupted. Reinstalling the driver will restore the sound.

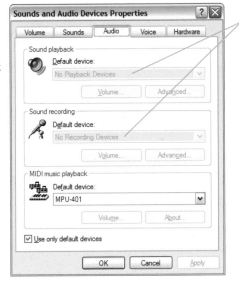

2 Click the Audio tab and if the Sound Playback & Sound Recording boxes are grayed out, then the sound system is not installed. Go to Step 4.

3 If the boxes are not grayed out, then the sound system is OK. Go to the next page.

4 Install the driver from the driver disk, then reboot the computer.

The Device Manager is the place to go when you are having problems with your hardware. Very often, the nature of a fault will be detailed here together with a solution.

In the unlikely event that you still have no sound after this, try checking for problems in the Device Manager. Go to Start, Control Panel, System, Hardware and Device Manager. Open the Sound, Video and Game Controllers category, locate the sound system or card, and see if there's a warning symbol next to it. If there is, right-click the device, click Properties, and the nature of the problem will be revealed in the next dialog box.

If you are using a sound card and Device Manager reports no problems, check that the card is firmly seated in its socket on the mainboard.

Then check that you have disabled the mainboard's integrated sound system – see page 165.

Finally, try a different card.

If the Sounds and Audio Devices Properties dialog box indicates that the sound system is correctly installed (Step 3, page 181), then check the system's volume level.

Click the Volume tab.

A common cause of lack of sound is simply connecting the speakers to the wrong sockets or to the wrong sound system.

If the slider is set to Low, drag it towards the High position.

If you are still not getting sound, check the speaker connections.

If you're using a sound card, make sure the speakers are actually connected to it and not to the integrated sound system. Also, make sure the speakers are connected to the correct jack, i.e. the "Speaker Out", "Audio Out" or "Line Out" jack.

If you are using an integrated sound system, the speakers will need a separate power supply. Make sure they are plugged in and that the speaker's volume control is turned up.

Finally, if you are using speakers that need their own power supply, make sure they are getting it and that the speaker volume control is turned up.

CD/DVD Drive has no Sound

If your CD/DVD drive is not producing any sound, the most likely reason is that you have forgotten to connect the drive's audio cable to the sound card – see page 132.

Also, check that the drive volume control in Windows is set high enough. Do this by going to Start, Control Panel, System, Hardware and Device Manager. Click the + sign next to DVD/CD-ROM Drives and then click your drive. Click the Properties tab, and under CD Player Volume, set the slider to an appropriate level.

Printers

All printers have the facility to print a test page, which is done with the printer isolated from the computer. The procedure varies from printer to printer. For instructions on how to carry out a printer test, refer to the instructions in your printer's documentation.

Printer Test Page

Refer to the manual for instructions on how to print a test page as the procedure varies from printer to printer. Usually, it will involve disconnecting the printer interface cable from the computer and then pressing a combination of buttons. If the test is successful, it establishes that the printer itself is ok and that the fault is either software-related or with the connections.

Printer Connections

Assuming the test page does print as it should, then the next thing to check is that the printer cables are ok and connected to the correct ports. It is unlikely that there will be anything wrong with the printer interface cable itself, but do check the connections to both the printer and the PC.

A potential cause of problems is having your printer connected to the computer via another device, using the Parallel Port. Any problems with the device could prevent the printer receiving data from the PC. Eliminate this possibility by connecting the printer directly to the computer.

Is the Printer Installed?

Go to Start, Control Panel and click Printers and Faxes.

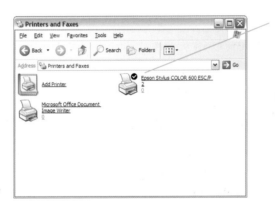

1 If your printer is installed you will see it here.

2 Make sure it is configured as the default printer (indicated by the black check mark).

The printer may have a resource conflict with another device. Check this out by going to Control Panel, System, Hardware, Device Manager, Ports (COM & LPT) and Printer Port (LPT1). Right-click LPT1, click Properties, and in the Printer Port Properties dialog box, click the Resources tab. In the Conflicting Device list at the bottom of the dialog box, check that there are no problems.

If the printer isn't installed, use its driver CD to install it via the Add Hardware wizard in the Control Panel.

Is the Printer using the Correct Port?

All printers use a specially designated port called LPT1; if your printer is not configured to use this port, it won't work.

Check this out by going to the Control Panel and clicking Printers and Faxes. Right-click the Printer icon and select Properties. Click the Ports tab, and if LPT1 hasn't been selected, do so by ticking the associated checkbox.

Scanners

SCSI scanners require the use of a SCSI adapter. These are usually supplied with the scanner in the form of a PCI card that must be installed in the PC. While these adapters are reliable enough, they do introduce another potential cause of problems.

Problems with scanners, particularly newly installed scanners, are usually related to incorrect connections and power issues.

Parallel Port Scanners

There are two issues likely to be experienced with these devices:

1) Connecting the scanner to the PC via the "Out" socket – these scanners have two Parallel Port sockets at the back (as shown in the picture below) – one for incoming data and one for outgoing data. You must use the "In" socket.

2) Connecting the scanner to the PC via another Parallel Port device such as a Zip drive or printer. Any problems with the other device will also prevent the scanner from working.

USB Powered Scanners

A common problem with some scanners is initialization failure. If you get an error message to this effect, try rebooting the computer while the scanner is switched on. This action initializes the scanner's internal settings, and on restart, it will usually work.

Most USB scanners draw their power from the USB interface. The problem with this is that the USB interface supplies a limited amount of power, and if a device attempts to draw more than this, it won't work. The usual problem is having more USB powered devices connected to the system than the interface can cope with. Check this out by disconnecting all other USB devices and trying the scanner again. If it now works, then you have been overloading the interface.

The only practical solution to this is to buy an AC powered USB hub. This device will supply all the power your USB devices need.

If you are using a USB scanner, make sure that USB has been enabled in the system's BIOS. See pages 164 – 165.

Initialization Failure

This is a common problem with scanners and will announce itself with a "Scanner Initialization Failed" error message. There are several causes of this: the scanner hasn't been connected to the system, it isn't powered up or you have selected the wrong driver in the scanning program. If none of these are causing the problem, however, leave the scanner switched on and reboot the PC. On restart, very often, the scanner will suddenly become operational.

Dial-up Modems

If the modem won't dial out, check the following:

Is it installed? – check to see that it is listed under the Modem category in Device Manager. If it isn't, reinstall the driver from the installation disk. If it still won't dial, you need to dig deeper.

Modem Diagnostic Check – open the Device Manager, locate the modem and right-click it. Select Properties. In the dialog box which opens, click the Diagnostics tab and then click "Query Modem".

If you get a "No Dial Tone" error message, check that you haven't simply forgotten to connect the cable linking the modem to the telephone socket.

1 If you see a list of "AT" commands, it indicates that the modem is working and that the problem is software related.

2 Go back to the Control Panel and click Network Connections. Right-click the modem connection and click Delete.

Modem drivers can be tricky things to install. If you have problems with yours, see if Windows XP will do the job for you. This operating system comes with a range of drivers for most types of peripherals.

Uninstall any modem driver you may have installed and reboot the system. On restart, Windows XP will "see" the modem, and if it has a compatible driver, will install it automatically.

3 Now reinstall the connection. If this was created with a CD from your ISP, then insert the disk and follow the instructions. Alternatively, you can use Windows XP's New Connection wizard.

If the modem now dials out, then the communications program was corrupt. If it still doesn't work, then the modem is almost certainly faulty.

If, however, the AT commands don't appear in the diagnostic test or you see a "Port Already In Use" message, then the modem is probably using the wrong COM port. Check the modem documentation to see which port it is designed to use. Then open Device Manager, right-click the modem and select Properties. Click the Advanced tab and then Advanced Port Settings. Check that the modem is set to the right port as per the documentation.

Broadband (Cable and DSL) Modems

If you cannot access the Internet via your broadband connection, the first thing to check is that the modem is communicating with the computer. You can do this by taking a look at the modem's front panel. Here, you will see a row of LEDs. Either the USB or ENET (Ethernet) LED should be lit (depending on the type of connection between the modem and computer).

Broadband modems have to go through an initialization routine before they become operational. This can take several minutes and is indicated by the LEDs flashing.

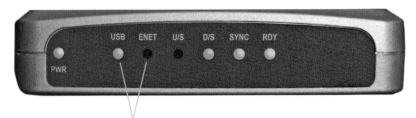

USB and Ethernet connection LEDs

If a LED indicates a problem, check that the connecting cable is fitted securely at both ends.

Then go to the Device Manager and check that there are no problems with the modem. This will be listed in the Network Adapter category.

If you are using a cable network, consider the possibility that the network itself is down. You can easily establish this by checking your TV – if it's not receiving a signal, then neither is the modem.

Alternatively, a phone call will quickly tell you what you need to know. Often, ISPs will play a recorded message detailing problem locations.

In the case of a USB connection, make sure that USB is enabled in the BIOS, as described on pages 164 – 165.

If you are using a cable modem, and it is connected via a signal splitter so that you can connect the incoming cable to another device such as a TV, remove the splitter and connect the modem directly to the cable.

If there is still no joy, then try resetting the modem. Many computer problems can be fixed by the simple expedient of switching off for a few seconds and then restarting. This applies equally to broadband modems. Some modems will have a reset button on the front panel for this purpose.

However, switching off the PC, disconnecting the modem and then reconnecting it before switching the PC back on again, is a better approach to take. Doing it this way can address a range of hardware and software issues.

Index